Editors
Kim Fields
Erica N. Russikoff, M.A.

Editor in Chief
Karen J. Goldfluss, M.S. Ed.

Illustrator
Vanessa Countryman

Cover Artist
Tony Carrillo

Art Coordinator
Renée Mc Elwee

Imaging
Rosa C. See

Publisher
Mary D. Smith, M.S. Ed.

Author
Mary Rosenberg

Correlations to the Common Core State Standards can be found at *http://www.teachercreated.com/standards/*.

Teacher Created Resources
6421 Industry Way
Westminster, CA 92683
www.teachercreated.com

ISBN: 978-1-4206-3576-8

Reprinted, 2013
Made in U.S.A.

Table of Contents

Introduction

Problem solving develops not only students' math skills but also their logical-thinking and abstract-thinking skills. Students need to be able to recognize the important elements in a problem, identify key words that tell which math operation(s) should be used, and know which problem-solving strategy is the best choice to answer the question. The student must also compare the answer(s) to the information presented in the problem. Does the answer make sense? Does it answer all parts of the question?

About this Book

The variety of math problems in *Daily Warm-Ups: Problem-Solving Math* will provide students with enough problem-solving practice to introduce your math period every day for an entire school year. For each warm-up, allow 10 to 15 minutes for reading, interpreting, and solving the problems. Students can work on the problems in this book independently, in groups, or as a whole class. Decide which approach works best for your students, based on their math skill levels and reading competence.

The book is divided into two sections. The first section of the book introduces four specific problem-solving strategies with math problems that are not directly addressed to a specific operation or concept. The math strategies are as follows: Drawing a Diagram, Creating a Table, Acting It Out or Using Concrete Materials, and Guessing and Checking. (See pages 8–12 for examples of math problems to which these types of strategies apply.) The second section of the book contains more traditional problems in operations, numeration, geometry, measurement, data analysis, probability, and algebra. The general math area and focus addressed in each warm-up is noted at the top of each page.

These activities can be used in a variety of ways, but they were designed to be introductory warm-ups for each math period. The 250 warm-ups are individually numbered and should be used in any order according to your main math lessons. Choose warm-ups that cover concepts previously taught so that the warm-up can serve as a review.

Some of the questions call for counters or manipulatives. These can be used to better understand math concepts. Plastic discs, cubes, and dry beans are examples of counters and manipulatives.

Standards

The math problems in this book have been correlated to the National Council of Teachers of Mathematics (NCTM) standards and the Common Core State Standards. See the correlation chart on pages 5–7. You will find the NCTM standards and expectations along with the warm-up numbers to which they relate. As the NCTM math standards make clear, problem solving is a critical component in math instruction. It is the component that makes general operations knowledge both essential and useful. Problem solving is the basic element in the concept of math as a method of communication.

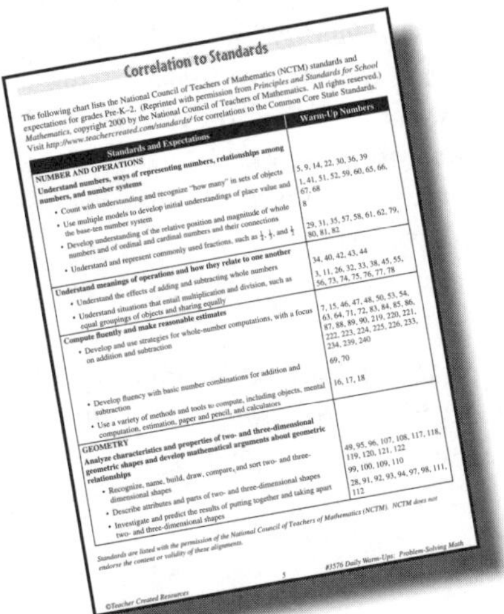

Correlation to Standards

The following chart lists the National Council of Teachers of Mathematics (NCTM) standards and expectations for grades Pre-K–2. (Reprinted with permission from *Principles and Standards for School Mathematics*, copyright 2000 by the National Council of Teachers of Mathematics. All rights reserved.) Visit *http://www.teachercreated.com/standards/* for correlations to the Common Core State Standards.

Standards and Expectations	Warm-Up Numbers
NUMBER AND OPERATIONS	
Understand numbers, ways of representing numbers, relationships among numbers, and number systems	
• Count with understanding and recognize "how many" in sets of objects	5, 9, 14, 22, 30, 36, 39
• Use multiple models to develop initial understandings of place value and the base-ten number system	1, 41, 51, 52, 59, 60, 65, 66, 67, 68
• Develop understanding of the relative position and magnitude of whole numbers and of ordinal and cardinal numbers and their connections	8
• Understand and represent commonly used fractions, such as $\frac{1}{4}$, $\frac{1}{3}$, and $\frac{1}{2}$	29, 31, 35, 57, 58, 61, 62, 79, 80, 81, 82
Understand meanings of operations and how they relate to one another	
• Understand the effects of adding and subtracting whole numbers	34, 40, 42, 43, 44
• Understand situations that entail multiplication and division, such as equal groupings of objects and sharing equally	3, 11, 26, 32, 33, 38, 45, 55, 56, 73, 74, 75, 76, 77, 78
Compute fluently and make reasonable estimates	
• Develop and use strategies for whole-number computations, with a focus on addition and subtraction	7, 15, 46, 47, 48, 50, 53, 54, 63, 64, 71, 72, 83, 84, 85, 86, 87, 88, 89, 90, 219, 220, 221, 222, 223, 224, 225, 226, 233, 234, 239, 240
• Develop fluency with basic number combinations for addition and subtraction	69, 70
• Use a variety of methods and tools to compute, including objects, mental computation, estimation, paper and pencil, and calculators	16, 17, 18
GEOMETRY	
Analyze characteristics and properties of two- and three-dimensional geometric shapes and develop mathematical arguments about geometric relationships	
• Recognize, name, build, draw, compare, and sort two- and three-dimensional shapes	49, 95, 96, 107, 108, 117, 118, 119, 120, 121, 122
• Describe attributes and parts of two- and three-dimensional shapes	99, 100, 109, 110
• Investigate and predict the results of putting together and taking apart two- and three-dimensional shapes	28, 91, 92, 93, 94, 97, 98, 111, 112

Standards are listed with the permission of the National Council of Teachers of Mathematics (NCTM). NCTM does not endorse the content or validity of these alignments.

©Teacher Created Resources 5 #3576 Daily Warm-Ups: Problem-Solving Math

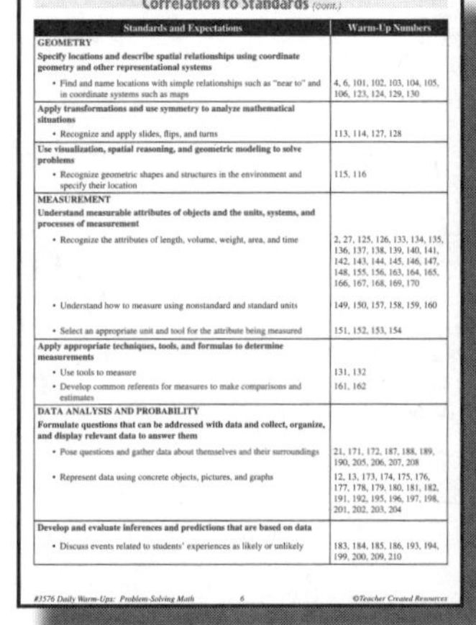

Correlation to Standards *(cont.)*

Standards and Expectations	Warm-Up Numbers
GEOMETRY	
Specify locations and describe spatial relationships using coordinate geometry and other representational systems	
• Find and name locations with simple relationships such as "near to" and in coordinate systems such as maps	4, 6, 101, 102, 103, 104, 105, 106, 123, 124, 129, 130
Apply transformations and use symmetry to analyze mathematical situations	
• Recognize and apply slides, flips, and turns	113, 114, 127, 128
Use visualization, spatial reasoning, and geometric modeling to solve problems	
• Recognize geometric shapes and structures in the environment and specify their location	115, 116
MEASUREMENT	
Understand measurable attributes of objects and the units, systems, and processes of measurement	
• Recognize the attributes of length, volume, weight, area, and time	2, 27, 125, 126, 133, 134, 135, 136, 137, 138, 139, 140, 141, 142, 143, 144, 145, 146, 147, 148, 155, 156, 163, 164, 165, 166, 167, 168, 169, 170
• Understand how to measure using nonstandard and standard units	149, 150, 157, 158, 159, 160
• Select an appropriate unit and tool for the attribute being measured	151, 152, 153, 154
Apply appropriate techniques, tools, and formulas to determine measurements	
• Use tools to measure	131, 132
• Develop common referents for measures to make comparisons and estimates	161, 162
DATA ANALYSIS AND PROBABILITY	
Formulate questions that can be addressed with data and collect, organize, and display relevant data to answer them	
• Pose questions and gather data about themselves and their surroundings	21, 171, 172, 187, 188, 189, 190, 205, 206, 207, 208
• Represent data using concrete objects, pictures, and graphs	12, 13, 173, 174, 175, 176, 177, 178, 179, 180, 181, 182, 191, 192, 195, 196, 197, 198, 201, 202, 203, 204
Develop and evaluate inferences and predictions that are based on data	
• Discuss events related to students' experiences as likely or unlikely	183, 184, 185, 186, 193, 194, 199, 200, 209, 210

#3576 Daily Warm-Ups: Problem-Solving Math 6 ©Teacher Created Resources

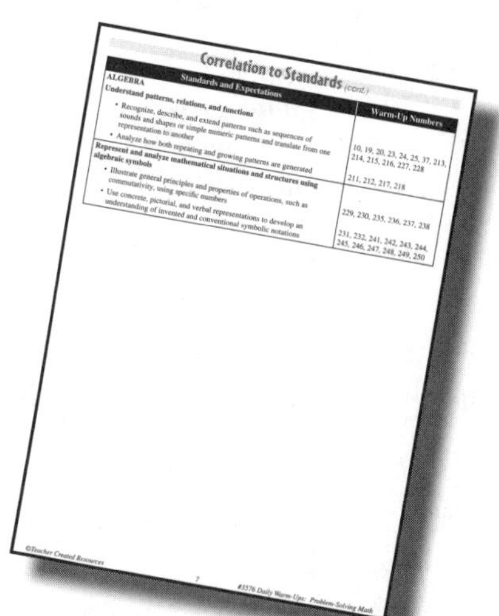

Correlation to Standards *(cont.)*

Standards and Expectations	Warm-Up Numbers
ALGEBRA	
Understand patterns, relations, and functions	
• Recognize, describe, and extend patterns such as sequences of sounds and shapes or simple numeric patterns and translate from one representation to another	10, 19, 20, 23, 24, 25, 37, 213, 214, 215, 216, 227, 228
• Analyze how both repeating and growing patterns are generated	211, 212, 217, 218
Represent and analyze mathematical situations and structures using algebraic symbols	
• Illustrate general principles and properties of operations, such as commutativity, using specific numbers	229, 230, 235, 236, 237, 238
• Use concrete, pictorial, and verbal representations to develop an understanding of invented and conventional symbolic notations	231, 232, 241, 242, 243, 244, 245, 246, 247, 248, 249, 250

Daily Warm-Ups, Section 1

The 50 warm-ups in this section follow one of four key problem-solving strategies. Each of these pages is set up the same way, allowing students to quickly become familiar with the expectations of the problems. The answers to the problems in this section have been provided along with explanations of the thinking process behind solving each one. (See pages 163–170 for Section 1's answers.)

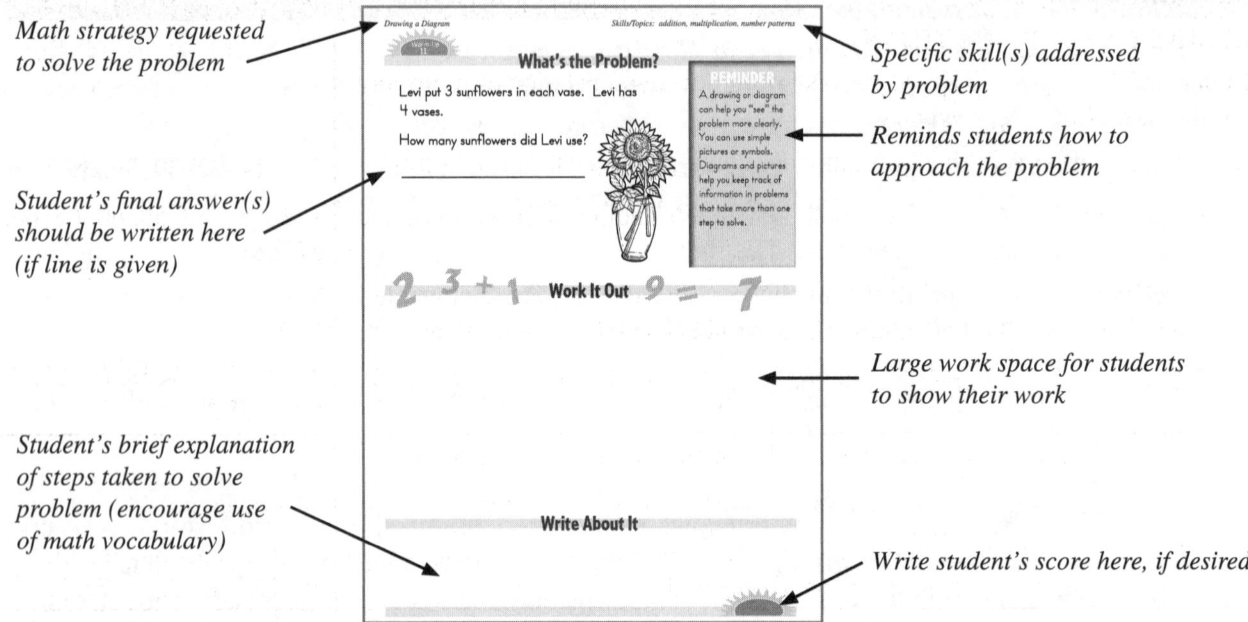

Daily Warm-Ups, Section 2

The 200 warm-ups in this section are divided into five math areas: Number and Operations, Geometry, Measurement, Data Analysis and Probability, and Algebra. Each of these pages has two warm-ups on the page. The two warm-ups relate to each other in some way. Warm-ups may be separated and given to students independently. Encourage students to apply math strategies as they solve the problems in this section.

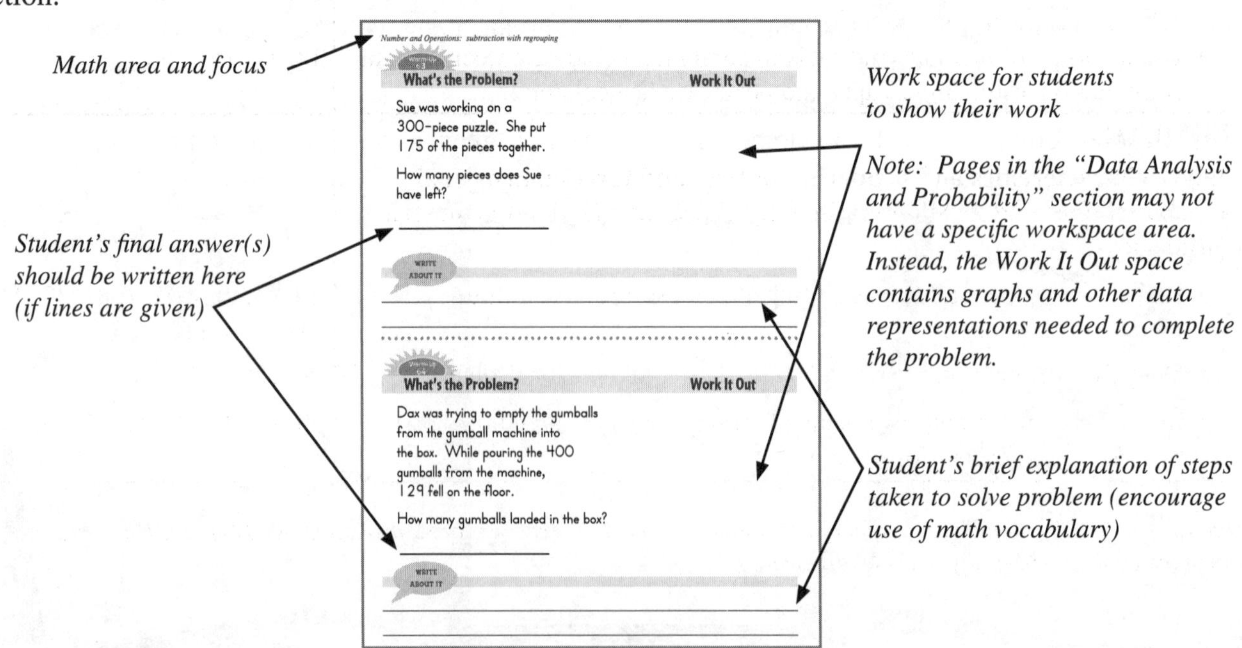

Correlation to Standards

The following chart lists the National Council of Teachers of Mathematics (NCTM) standards and expectations for grades Pre-K–2. (Reprinted with permission from *Principles and Standards for School Mathematics,* copyright 2000 by the National Council of Teachers of Mathematics. All rights reserved.) Visit *http://www.teachercreated.com/standards/* for correlations to the Common Core State Standards.

Standards and Expectations	Warm-Up Numbers
NUMBER AND OPERATIONS	
Understand numbers, ways of representing numbers, relationships among numbers, and number systems	
• Count with understanding and recognize "how many" in sets of objects	5, 9, 14, 22, 30, 36, 39
• Use multiple models to develop initial understandings of place value and the base-ten number system	1, 41, 51, 52, 59, 60, 65, 66, 67, 68
• Develop understanding of the relative position and magnitude of whole numbers and of ordinal and cardinal numbers and their connections	8
• Understand and represent commonly used fractions, such as $\frac{1}{4}$, $\frac{1}{3}$, and $\frac{1}{2}$	29, 31, 35, 57, 58, 61, 62, 79, 80, 81, 82
Understand meanings of operations and how they relate to one another	
• Understand the effects of adding and subtracting whole numbers	34, 40, 42, 43, 44
• Understand situations that entail multiplication and division, such as equal groupings of objects and sharing equally	3, 11, 26, 32, 33, 38, 45, 55, 56, 73, 74, 75, 76, 77, 78
Compute fluently and make reasonable estimates	
• Develop and use strategies for whole-number computations, with a focus on addition and subtraction	7, 15, 46, 47, 48, 50, 53, 54, 63, 64, 71, 72, 83, 84, 85, 86, 87, 88, 89, 90, 219, 220, 221, 222, 223, 224, 225, 226, 233, 234, 239, 240
• Develop fluency with basic number combinations for addition and subtraction	69, 70
• Use a variety of methods and tools to compute, including objects, mental computation, estimation, paper and pencil, and calculators	16, 17, 18
GEOMETRY	
Analyze characteristics and properties of two- and three-dimensional geometric shapes and develop mathematical arguments about geometric relationships	
• Recognize, name, build, draw, compare, and sort two- and three-dimensional shapes	49, 95, 96, 107, 108, 117, 118, 119, 120, 121, 122
• Describe attributes and parts of two- and three-dimensional shapes	99, 100, 109, 110
• Investigate and predict the results of putting together and taking apart two- and three-dimensional shapes	28, 91, 92, 93, 94, 97, 98, 111, 112

Standards are listed with the permission of the National Council of Teachers of Mathematics (NCTM). NCTM does not endorse the content or validity of these alignments.

Correlation to Standards *(cont.)*

Standards and Expectations	Warm-Up Numbers
GEOMETRY	
Specify locations and describe spatial relationships using coordinate geometry and other representational systems	
• Find and name locations with simple relationships such as "near to" and in coordinate systems such as maps	4, 6, 101, 102, 103, 104, 105, 106, 123, 124, 129, 130
Apply transformations and use symmetry to analyze mathematical situations	
• Recognize and apply slides, flips, and turns	113, 114, 127, 128
Use visualization, spatial reasoning, and geometric modeling to solve problems	
• Recognize geometric shapes and structures in the environment and specify their location	115, 116
MEASUREMENT	
Understand measurable attributes of objects and the units, systems, and processes of measurement	
• Recognize the attributes of length, volume, weight, area, and time	2, 27, 125, 126, 133, 134, 135, 136, 137, 138, 139, 140, 141, 142, 143, 144, 145, 146, 147, 148, 155, 156, 163, 164, 165, 166, 167, 168, 169, 170
• Understand how to measure using nonstandard and standard units	149, 150, 157, 158, 159, 160
• Select an appropriate unit and tool for the attribute being measured	151, 152, 153, 154
Apply appropriate techniques, tools, and formulas to determine measurements	
• Use tools to measure	131, 132
• Develop common referents for measures to make comparisons and estimates	161, 162
DATA ANALYSIS AND PROBABILITY	
Formulate questions that can be addressed with data and collect, organize, and display relevant data to answer them	
• Pose questions and gather data about themselves and their surroundings	21, 171, 172, 187, 188, 189, 190, 205, 206, 207, 208
• Represent data using concrete objects, pictures, and graphs	12, 13, 173, 174, 175, 176, 177, 178, 179, 180, 181, 182, 191, 192, 195, 196, 197, 198, 201, 202, 203, 204
Develop and evaluate inferences and predictions that are based on data	
• Discuss events related to students' experiences as likely or unlikely	183, 184, 185, 186, 193, 194, 199, 200, 209, 210

Correlation to Standards *(cont.)*

Standards and Expectations	Warm-Up Numbers
ALGEBRA	
Understand patterns, relations, and functions	
• Recognize, describe, and extend patterns such as sequences of sounds and shapes or simple numeric patterns and translate from one representation to another	10, 19, 20, 23, 24, 25, 37, 213, 214, 215, 216, 227, 228
• Analyze how both repeating and growing patterns are generated	211, 212, 217, 218
Represent and analyze mathematical situations and structures using algebraic symbols	
• Illustrate general principles and properties of operations, such as commutativity, using specific numbers	229, 230, 235, 236, 237, 238
• Use concrete, pictorial, and verbal representations to develop an understanding of invented and conventional symbolic notations	231, 232, 241, 242, 243, 244, 245, 246, 247, 248, 249, 250

Examples of Strategies

Drawing a Diagram

Drawing a diagram or picture can help you "see" a problem more clearly. Diagrams and pictures help you keep track of information in problems that take more than one step to solve. When drawing one, make sure all elements of the problem are included.

Example 1

What's the Problem?

Three classmates were standing in a line. Sabrina is in between Charlie and Chelsea. Chelsea is first.

What is the order of the classmates?

____

Work It Out

Chelsea

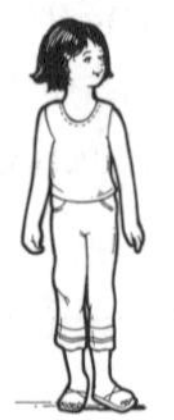
Sabrina

Charlie

Write About It

To solve the problem, a student might draw a picture of the classmates, using the order given in the problem. The student would then answer the question by recording the order of the classmates.

Drawing a diagram or picture can help show directions.

Example 2

What's the Problem?

Fido wanted to bury his favorite dog bone in a safe spot. He left his doghouse and walked 4 feet east, 3 feet north, 2 feet west, and 1 foot south.

How many feet did Fido walk?

$4 + 3 + 2 + 1 = 10$

Work It Out

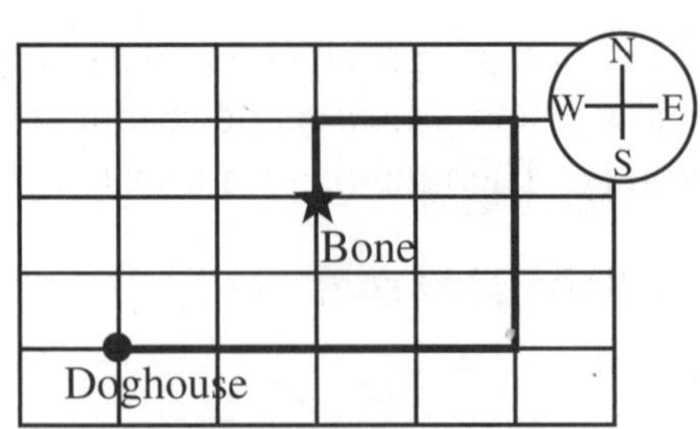

Each square = 1 foot

Write About It

To solve the problem, a student might draw a grid, where each square equals 1 foot. The student would then follow Fido's route and calculate the number of feet walked to answer the question.

Examples of Strategies *(cont.)*

Drawing a Diagram *(cont.)*

Drawing a diagram or picture can show how an item has been shared.

Example 3

What's the Problem?

Mark has 20 marbles. He shares half with his brother, Tony. Tony gives 5 marbles to a friend and keeps the rest.

How many marbles does each boy have?

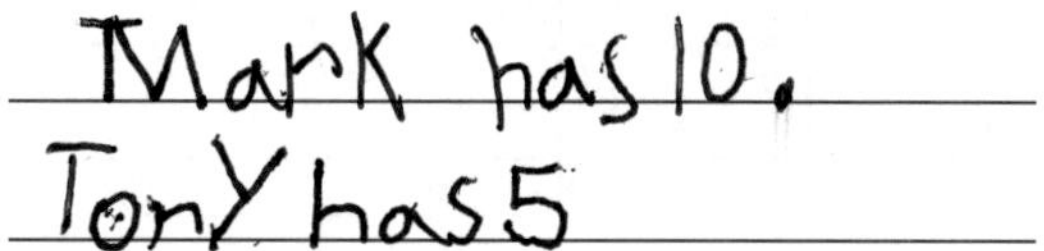

Work It Out

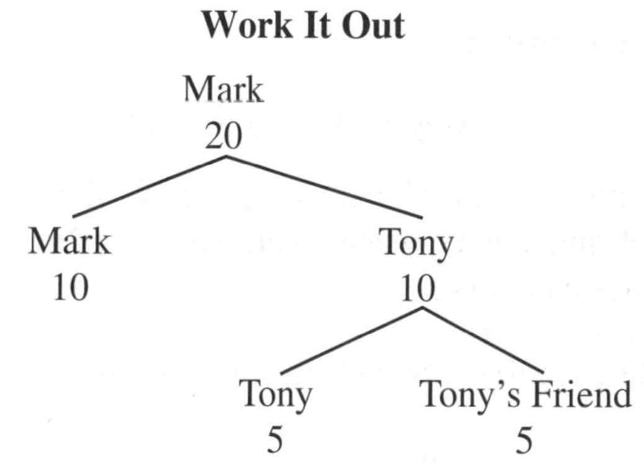

Write About It

To solve the problem, a student might draw a diagram of the marble disbursement between Mark, Tony, and Tony's friend. The student would then answer the question by recording the total number of marbles for each person.

Drawing a diagram or picture can show an intricate pattern.

Example 4

What's the Problem?

Marta is drawing a pattern on a piece of paper. She makes 1 star, 2 hearts, 1 circle, and 2 diamonds. Then the pattern repeats.

What will the 23rd shape be?

diamonds

Work It Out

Write About It

To solve the problem, a student might draw Marta's pattern. The student would then answer the question after reaching the 23rd shape.

Creating a Table

Creating a table helps you organize and keep track of information. A table makes it easy to see the relationships and patterns among sets of numbers. When making a table, decide which information needs to be shown, how many columns and rows are needed, and what the headings (titles) should be. Remember to work in order and list all combinations.

Example 1

What's the Problem?

Using nickels, dimes, and quarters, how many different ways can Sylvia make 25 cents?

Work It Out

Number of Ways	Number of Nickels	Number of Dimes	Number of Quarters
1	0	0	1
2	1	2	0
3	3	1	0
4	5	0	0

Write About It

To solve the problem, a student might create a table showing the different coin combinations that amount to 25 cents. The student would then answer the question by recording the number of coin combinations (ways).

Creating a table can show comparisons between pieces of information.

Example 2

What's the Problem?

Mona reads 12 pages from a book each night. Nicole reads 9 pages from a book each night.

On what day will Nicole finish reading 72 pages? ____________

How many pages will Mona have read?

____

Work It Out

Day Number	Pages Read—Mona	Pages Read—Nicole
1	12	9
2	24	18
3	36	27
4	48	36
5	60	45
6	72	54
7	84	63
8	96	72

Write About It

To solve the problem, a student might create a table, filling in the information until the first answer is found. The student would then answer the second question by comparing Nicole's pages read to Mona's pages read.

Examples of Strategies *(cont.)*

Acting It Out or Using Concrete Materials

Acting it out or using concrete materials is helpful when it is difficult to visualize the problem or hard to figure out the procedure. Use real objects to create a model or use people to act out the problem and its solution. By acting it out or using objects to represent parts of the problem, you can "see" its solution better.

Example 1

What's the Problem?

Barb has a jar filled with 20 black cubes. Barb takes out 5 black cubes and puts in 10 white cubes. Barb takes out 5 more black cubes and puts in 10 more white cubes.

How many cubes are in the jar? 30

How many of the cubes are black and how many of the cubes are white?

b10 W20

Work It Out

Write About It

To solve the problem, a student might use a jar filled with black and white cubes. After following the directions provided in the problem, the student would see the answers to the questions.

Using concrete materials can be helpful when comparing quantities.

Example 2

What's the Problem?

Pat needs to solve this math problem.

Which is more: 3 rows of 8 cubes or 2 rows of 10 cubes?

3 rows of 24

Work It Out

Write About It

To solve the problem, a student might use cubes or other manipulatives. The student would lay out the rows of cubes into two sets and compare the quantities.

Examples of Strategies *(cont.)*

Guessing and Checking

Guessing and checking helps you develop reasonable guesses to solve a problem. For each guess, look at the important information presented in the problem. Check each guess against the information. Base the next guess on the previous result. Use a table to help organize your guesses.

Example 1

What's the Problem?

On the field trip, there were twice as many girls as adults. There were three times as many boys as adults. There were 30 people in all.

How many adults, girls, and boys went on the field trip?

____

____

Work It Out

Guess Number	1	2	3	4	5
Adults	1	8	3	6	5
Girls	2	16	6	12	10
Boys	3	24	9	18	15
Total People	6	48	18	36	30

Write About It

To solve the problem, a student might create a table to show the varied numbers of adults, girls, and boys. The student would continue to guess and check until reaching 30, which is the total number of people on the field trip (provided in the question).

Guessing and checking can be used when the answer is provided.

Example 2

What's the Problem?

Elliott and Savannah have 12 guinea pigs. Elliott has two more guinea pigs than Savannah.

How many guinea pigs does each one have?

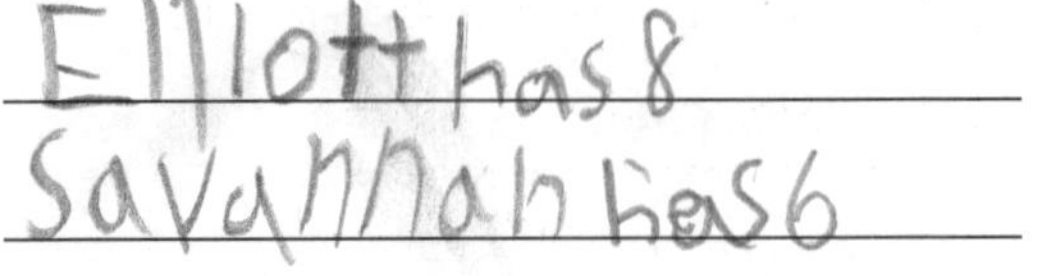

Work It Out

Guess Number	1	2
Savannah's Guinea Pigs	6	5
Elliott's Guinea Pigs	8	7
Total Guinea Pigs	14	12

Write About It

To solve the problem, a student might create a table to compare the number of guinea pigs for each person. The student would continue to guess and check until reaching 12, which is the total number of guinea pigs (provided in the question).

What's the Problem?

Use the hundreds chart to find the mystery number.

- The number has 2 even digits.
- The number in the tens place is greater than the number in the ones place.
- The sum of both digits is 12.

What is the mystery number? Circle it below.

REMINDER

A drawing or diagram can help you "see" the problem more clearly. You can use simple pictures or symbols. Diagrams and pictures help you keep track of information in problems that take more than one step to solve.

Work It Out

1	2	3	4	5	6	7	8	9	10
11	12	13	14	15	16	17	18	19	20
21	22	23	24	25	26	27	28	29	30
31	32	33	34	35	36	37	38	39	40
41	42	43	44	45	46	47	48	49	50
51	52	53	54	55	56	57	58	59	60
61	62	63	64	65	66	67	68	69	70
71	72	73	74	75	76	77	78	79	80
81	82	83	84	85	86	87	88	89	90
91	92	93	94	95	96	97	98	99	100

Write About It

Warm-Up 2

What's the Problem?

Avonlea has homework 4 nights each week. (Monday—Thursday)

How many nights will Avonlea have homework this month?

4+4+4+4=16

REMINDER

A drawing or diagram can help you "see" the problem more clearly. You can use simple pictures or symbols. Diagrams and pictures help you keep track of information in problems that take more than one step to solve.

Work It Out

April

SUNDAY	MONDAY	TUESDAY	WEDNESDAY	THURSDAY	FRIDAY	SATURDAY
					1	2
3	4	5	6	7	8	9
10	11	12	13	14	15	16
17	18	19	20	21	22	23
24	25	26	27	28	29	30

Write About It

What's the Problem?

Tara drew a star and counted 5 points.

If Tara drew 8 stars, how many points would there be in all?

40 Points

REMINDER

A drawing or diagram can help you "see" the problem more clearly. You can use simple pictures or symbols. Diagrams and pictures help you keep track of information in problems that take more than one step to solve.

Work It Out

Write About It

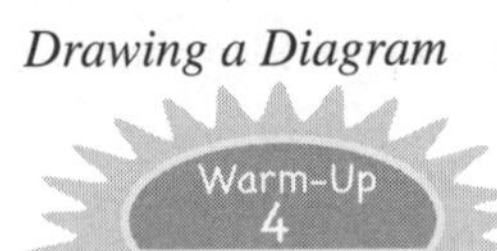

What's the Problem?

The teacher made a seating chart for 5 students: Tad, Fred, Amy, Tiffany, and Phil.

- Tad is in the first seat.
- Phil is behind Tad but before Tiffany.
- Tiffany is in between Phil and Amy.
- Fred is last.

Where is each person's seat?

REMINDER

A drawing or diagram can help you "see" the problem more clearly. You can use simple pictures or symbols. Diagrams and pictures help you keep track of information in problems that take more than one step to solve.

Work It Out

Tad	Phil	Tiffany	Amy	Fred
1st	**2nd**	**3rd**	**4th**	**5th**

Write About It

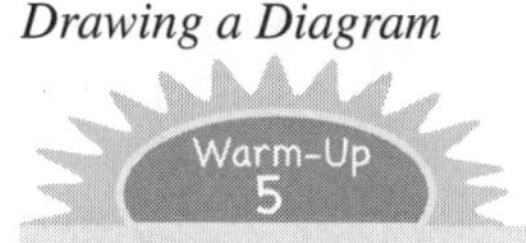

What's the Problem?

Drew is painting the fence in her backyard. Drew is painting the fence white, but every 6th board will be painted green. The fence has 50 boards.

How many green boards will Drew paint?

8 ____________

REMINDER

A drawing or diagram can help you "see" the problem more clearly. You can use simple pictures or symbols. Diagrams and pictures help you keep track of information in problems that take more than one step to solve.

Work It Out

Write About It

Warm-Up 6

What's the Problem?

Sage drew a map of the school.

- The kindergarten classroom is north of the office.
- The playground is east of the kindergarten classroom.
- The lunchroom is south of the office.
- The bus zone is west of the office.
- The primary classrooms are east of the office.
- The upper-grade classrooms are north of the bus zone.

What does Sage's map look like? Draw it below.

REMINDER

A drawing or diagram can help you "see" the problem more clearly. You can use simple pictures or symbols. Diagrams and pictures help you keep track of information in problems that take more than one step to solve.

Work It Out

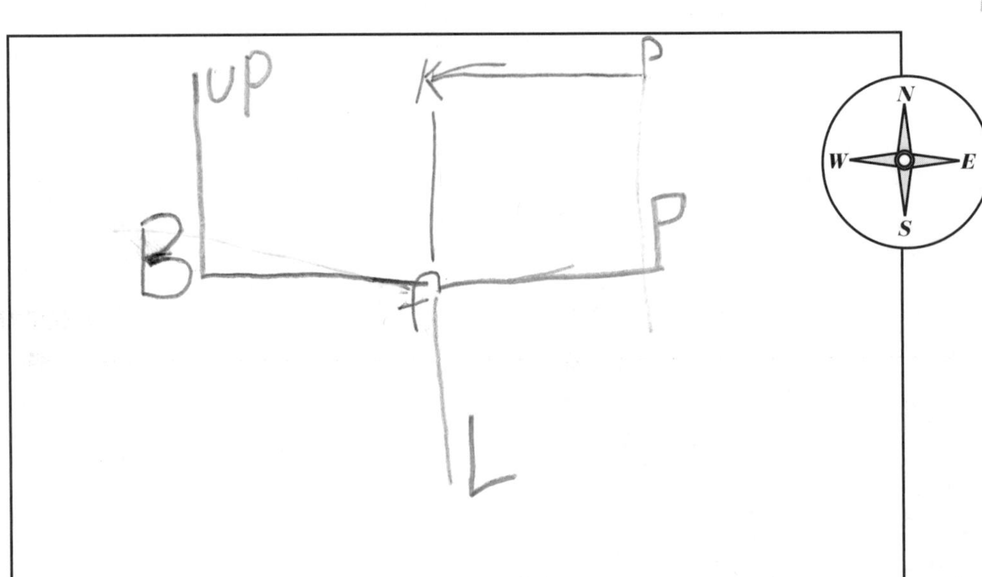

Write About It

What's the Problem?

Cindy's home, school, and library are all on the same street. Cindy's home is at one end of the street, and the library is at the other end of the street.

One day, Cindy walked 2 blocks from home to school. Then she walked 3 blocks from school to the library and from the library back home.

How many blocks did Cindy walk in all?

2+3=5
____

REMINDER

A drawing or diagram can help you "see" the problem more clearly. You can use simple pictures or symbols. Diagrams and pictures help you keep track of information in problems that take more than one step to solve.

Work It Out

Write About It

What's the Problem?

Twenty animals were placed in a circle.

- Every fifth animal is a duck.
- Every sixth animal is a goose.
- The remaining animals are foxes.

How many of each animal are there?

4Foxs 3Ducks

3Gees

REMINDER

A drawing or diagram can help you "see" the problem more clearly. You can use simple pictures or symbols. Diagrams and pictures help you keep track of information in problems that take more than one step to solve.

Work It Out

Write About It

What's the Problem?

How many dots are on a 6-sided die?

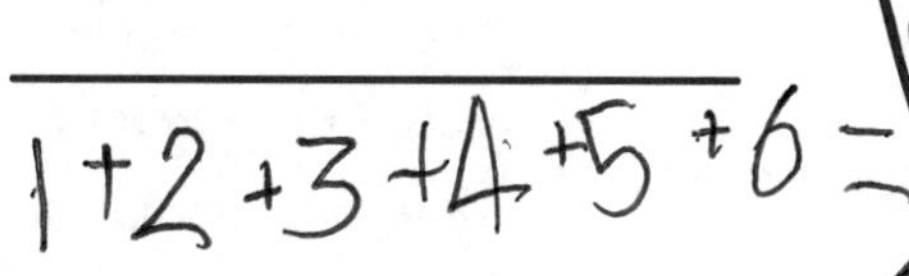

REMINDER

A drawing or diagram can help you "see" the problem more clearly. You can use simple pictures or symbols. Diagrams and pictures help you keep track of information in problems that take more than one step to solve.

Work It Out

Write About It

Warm-Up 10

What's the Problem?

Candy is stacking bricks. She puts 1 brick in the first column, 2 bricks in the second column, and 3 bricks in the third column.

If Candy continues this pattern, how many bricks will she use to make 10 columns?

55 Bricks

REMINDER

A drawing or diagram can help you "see" the problem more clearly. You can use simple pictures or symbols. Diagrams and pictures help you keep track of information in problems that take more than one step to solve.

Work It Out

Write About It

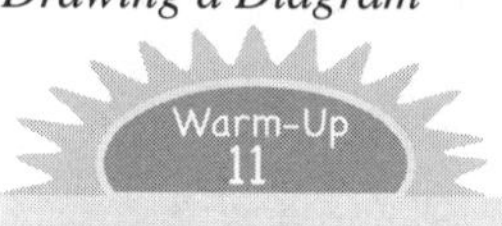

What's the Problem?

Levi put 3 sunflowers in each vase. Levi has 4 vases.

How many sunflowers did Levi use?

Levi has 12 sunflowers

REMINDER

A drawing or diagram can help you "see" the problem more clearly. You can use simple pictures or symbols. Diagrams and pictures help you keep track of information in problems that take more than one step to solve.

Work It Out

Write About It

What's the Problem?

Rosa has 3 pennies.

If she flipped the pennies, how many different ways could the pennies land?

2 flips

REMINDER

A drawing or diagram can help you "see" the problem more clearly. You can use simple pictures or symbols. Diagrams and pictures help you keep track of information in problems that take more than one step to solve.

Work It Out

Write About It

What's the Problem?

Beth is at the Scarf Shop. She wants to make her own scarf.

How many different scarves could Beth make?

____

Ends	Fleece
Straight	Solid
Fringed	Striped

REMINDER

A drawing or diagram can help you "see" the problem more clearly. You can use simple pictures or symbols. Diagrams and pictures help you keep track of information in problems that take more than one step to solve.

Work It Out

Write About It

What's the Problem?

The school bus has 15 seats. Each seat can hold 2 students or 1 adult.

How many seats will be used for a class of 24 students and 3 adults?

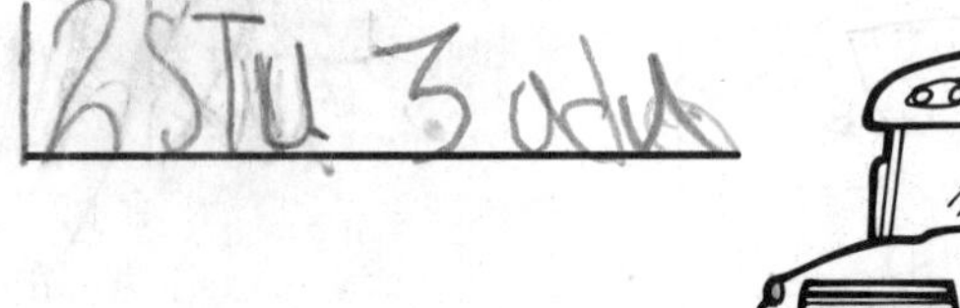

REMINDER

A drawing or diagram can help you "see" the problem more clearly. You can use simple pictures or symbols. Diagrams and pictures help you keep track of information in problems that take more than one step to solve.

Work It Out

Write About It

What's the Problem?

Marva has pennies, nickels, dimes, and quarters.

Using at least 1 of each coin, list 8 different ways that Marva can make 75 cents.

Use the table to help you.

REMINDER

Creating a table helps you organize information. Follow these steps:

1. Work in order and list all combinations.
2. Keep one item the same while others change.
3. Fill in any gaps.
4. Record the solution so it is easy to understand.

Work It Out

Number of Pennies	Number of Nickels	Number of Dimes	Number of Quarters	Total Value
75P				

Write About It

What's the Problem?

Evan is 6 years old. His sister, Rachel, is 15 years old.

How old will they both be when Evan is half as old as his sister?

Creating a table helps you organize information. Follow these steps:

1. Work in order and list all combinations.
2. Keep one item the same while others change.
3. Fill in any gaps.
4. Record the solution so it is easy to understand.

Work It Out

Evan's Age	Rachel's Age
6 years old	15 years old

Write About It

What's the Problem?

There are 21 students in the class. There are twice as many boys as girls.

How many boys and girls are in the class?

REMINDER

Creating a table helps you organize information. Follow these steps:

1. Work in order and list all combinations.
2. Keep one item the same while others change.
3. Fill in any gaps.
4. Record the solution so it is easy to understand.

Work It Out

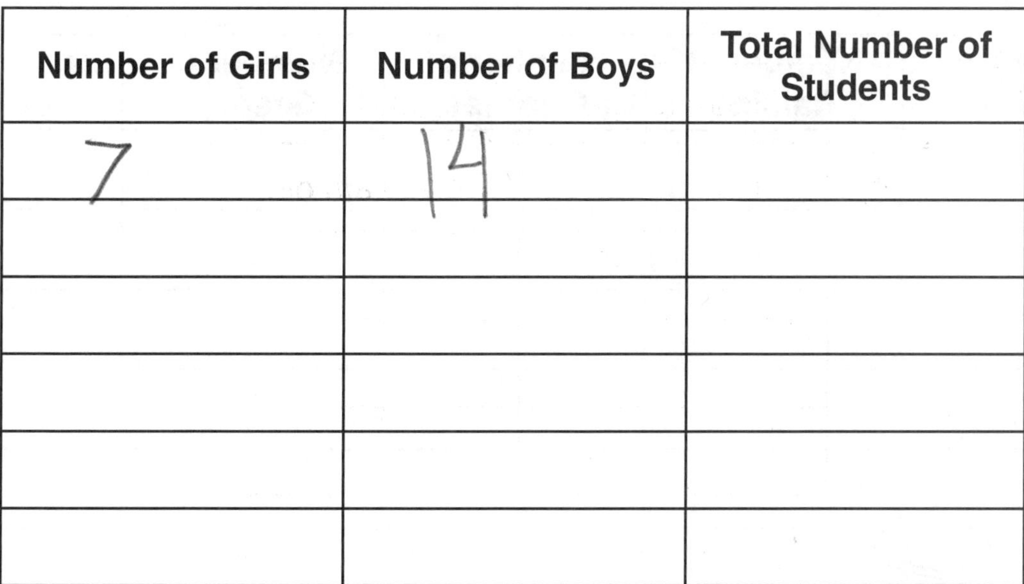

Number of Girls	Number of Boys	Total Number of Students
7	14	

Write About It

What's the Problem?

This fruit salad has raisins, grapes, and cherries. Each serving of fruit salad has: 1 raisin, 2 cherries, and 4 grapes.

How many fruit salads can be made with 21 pieces of fruit?

3 Salad ______________

REMINDER

Creating a table helps you organize information. Follow these steps:

1. Work in order and list all combinations.
2. Keep one item the same while others change.
3. Fill in any gaps.
4. Record the solution so it is easy to understand.

Work It Out

Number of Salads	Number of Raisins	Number of Cherries	Number of Grapes	Total Pieces of Fruit

Write About It

What's the Problem?

Dean has taken up running. The first week, he runs for 10 minutes. Each week, he increases his time by 4 minutes.

How many weeks before Dean is able to run for 30 minutes?

6 weeks

REMINDER

Creating a table helps you organize information. Follow these steps:

1. Work in order and list all combinations.
2. Keep one item the same while others change.
3. Fill in any gaps.
4. Record the solution so it is easy to understand.

Work It Out

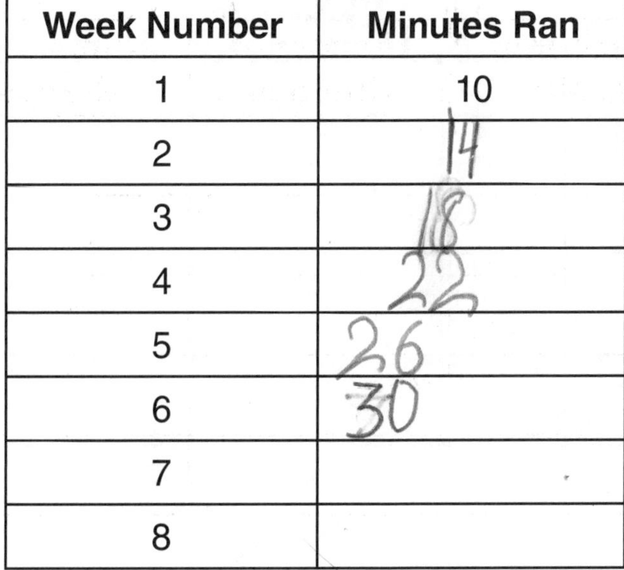

Week Number	Minutes Ran
1	10
2	14
3	18
4	22
5	26
6	30
7	
8	

Write About It

What's the Problem?

Each tricycle has 3 wheels.

How many wheels are on 8 tricycles?

24 Wheels

REMINDER

Creating a table helps you organize information. Follow these steps:

1. Work in order and list all combinations.
2. Keep one item the same while others change.
3. Fill in any gaps.
4. Record the solution so it is easy to understand.

2 3 + 1 Work It Out 9 = 7

Number of Tricycles	1	2	3	4	5	6	7	8
Number of Wheels	3	6	9	12	15	18	21	24

Write About It

What's the Problem?

Alex ordered a triple scoop ice-cream cone. He ordered a scoop of vanilla, a scoop of chocolate, and a scoop of strawberry.

How many different ways could the scoops be stacked?

4 ________________

REMINDER

Creating a table helps you organize information. Follow these steps:

1. Work in order and list all combinations.
2. Keep one item the same while others change.
3. Fill in any gaps.
4. Record the solution so it is easy to understand.

Work It Out

1st Scoop	2nd Scoop	3rd Scoop
Vanilla	Chocolate	Straberry
V	St	Ch
St	V	Ch
Ch	S	V

Write About It

What's the Problem?

The Pet Store sells hamsters, parrots, and rabbits.

- There are 2 more parrots than hamsters.
- There are 3 more rabbits than parrots.
- There are 25 pets in all.

How many hamsters, parrots, and rabbits does the Pet Store have?

____

____

REMINDER

Creating a table helps you organize information. Follow these steps:

1. Work in order and list all combinations.
2. Keep one item the same while others change.
3. Fill in any gaps.
4. Record the solution so it is easy to understand.

Work It Out

Number of Hamsters	Number of Parrots	Number of Rabbits	Total Number of Animals

Write About It

What's the Problem?

Travis used the Number Machine. For each number Travis put into the machine, a different number came out.

What are the missing numbers? Complete the table.

What is the rule?

____

____

REMINDER

Creating a table helps you organize information. Follow these steps:

1. Work in order and list all combinations.
2. Keep one item the same while others change.
3. Fill in any gaps.
4. Record the solution so it is easy to understand.

Work It Out

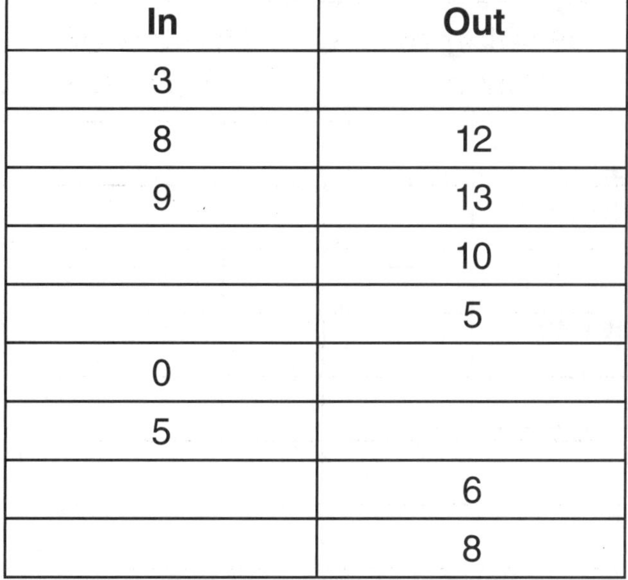

In	Out
3	
8	12
9	13
	10
	5
0	
5	
	6
	8

Write About It

What's the Problem?

Fans are lining up for the baseball game. The ticket lady first lets in 1 person, then a group of 4 people. Each group increases by 3 people.

How many people will be in the fifth group?

____

REMINDER

Creating a table helps you organize information. Follow these steps:

1. Work in order and list all combinations.
2. Keep one item the same while others change.
3. Fill in any gaps.
4. Record the solution so it is easy to understand.

Work It Out

Person or Group Number	1	2	3	4	5
Number of People					

Write About It

What's the Problem?

Barney ate 75 bones in 5 days. Each day, he ate 7 more bones than he had the previous day.

How many bones did he eat each day?

Complete the table to find out.

REMINDER

Creating a table helps you organize information. Follow these steps:

1. Work in order and list all combinations.
2. Keep one item the same while others change.
3. Fill in any gaps.
4. Record the solution so it is easy to understand.

Work It Out

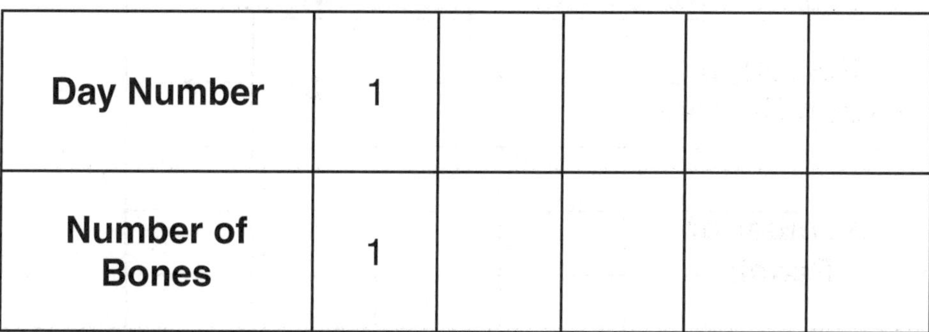

Day Number	1				
Number of Bones	1				

Write About It

What's the Problem?

The principal is ordering new swing sets. Each swing set has 3 swings.

How many swing sets should the principal order so that 16 students can use the swings at the same time?

____

REMINDER

Creating a table helps you organize information. Follow these steps:

1. Work in order and list all combinations.
2. Keep one item the same while others change.
3. Fill in any gaps.
4. Record the solution so it is easy to understand.

Work It Out

Number of Swing Sets	Number of Swings

Write About It

What's the Problem?

This picture shows 5 counters.

Will more than 50 counters fit in your pencil box?

____

REMINDER

Sometimes a problem is hard to picture or to solve. Use real objects to make a model or use people (or objects) to act out the problem.

By acting it out, talking through the problem, or using objects, you can "see" its solution better.

Work It Out

Write About It

What's the Problem?

David has 5 squares.

Show the different ways that David can arrange the squares so that they all touch each other on at least 1 side.

REMINDER

Sometimes a problem is hard to picture or to solve. Use real objects to make a model or use people (or objects) to act out the problem.

By acting it out, talking through the problem, or using objects, you can "see" its solution better.

Work It Out

Write About It

What's the Problem?

Antonio has 10 pencils. His brother has half as many pencils as Antonio.

How many pencils do the brothers have in all?

____

REMINDER

Sometimes a problem is hard to picture or to solve. Use real objects to make a model or use people (or objects) to act out the problem.

By acting it out, talking through the problem, or using objects, you can "see" its solution better.

Work It Out

Write About It

What's the Problem?

How many 1's are there on the face of an analog clock?

REMINDER

Sometimes a problem is hard to picture or to solve. Use real objects to make a model or use people (or objects) to act out the problem.

By acting it out, talking through the problem, or using objects, you can "see" its solution better.

Work It Out

Write About It

What's the Problem?

Marcy folds a square piece of paper in half. She does this 3 more times.

How many squares will Marcy have after 4 folds?

____

REMINDER

Sometimes a problem is hard to picture or to solve. Use real objects to make a model or use people (or objects) to act out the problem.

By acting it out, talking through the problem, or using objects, you can "see" its solution better.

Work It Out

Write About It

What's the Problem?

Jeremiah cut a 12-inch piece of string into 3 equal lengths.

How long is each piece?

____

How many cuts did Jeremiah make?

____

REMINDER

Sometimes a problem is hard to picture or to solve. Use real objects to make a model or use people (or objects) to act out the problem.

By acting it out, talking through the problem, or using objects, you can "see" its solution better.

Work It Out

Write About It

What's the Problem?

Joanne wants to share 9 cookies with 3 friends.

Including Joanne, how many cookies will each person get?

____

How many cookies will be left over?

____

REMINDER

Sometimes a problem is hard to picture or to solve. Use real objects to make a model or use people (or objects) to act out the problem.

By acting it out, talking through the problem, or using objects, you can "see" its solution better.

Work It Out

Write About It

What's the Problem?

Sela has 19 counters.

If she takes 3 away at a time, will she end up with 0 counters?

____

REMINDER

Sometimes a problem is hard to picture or to solve. Use real objects to make a model or use people (or objects) to act out the problem.

By acting it out, talking through the problem, or using objects, you can "see" its solution better.

Work It Out

Write About It

What's the Problem?

Mark made a large pizza.

How many straight cuts across the pizza will he make for 8 equal slices?

____

REMINDER

Sometimes a problem is hard to picture or to solve. Use real objects to make a model or use people (or objects) to act out the problem.

By acting it out, talking through the problem, or using objects, you can "see" its solution better.

Work It Out

Write About It

What's the Problem?

Bettina wrote the numbers 1 to 20.

How many odd numbers did Bettina write?

____

REMINDER

Sometimes a problem is hard to picture or to solve. Use real objects to make a model or use people (or objects) to act out the problem.

By acting it out, talking through the problem, or using objects, you can "see" its solution better.

Work It Out

Write About It

What's the Problem?

Molly has a deck of playing cards. She places 7 cards in a row on the table. Starting with the second card, Molly places another card on top of the remaining cards. Molly repeats this step starting with the third card.

If Molly continues this pattern, how many cards will be in the last stack? ___________

How many cards will Molly use in all? __________

REMINDER

Sometimes a problem is hard to picture or to solve. Use real objects to make a model or use people (or objects) to act out the problem.

By acting it out, talking through the problem, or using objects, you can "see" its solution better.

Work It Out

Write About It

What's the Problem?

Wally had 25 jelly beans. He put them in 5 equal groups.

How many jelly beans did Wally put in each group?

____

REMINDER

Sometimes a problem is hard to picture or to solve. Use real objects to make a model or use people (or objects) to act out the problem.

By acting it out, talking through the problem, or using objects, you can "see" its solution better.

Work It Out

Write About It

What's the Problem?

Zoe the Zookeeper counts feet to keep track of the zebras and the flamingos at the zoo.

- There are 3 more flamingos than zebras.
- There are the same number of flamingo legs as zebra legs.

How many flamingos and zebras did Zoe count?

____

Use the table below if needed.

REMINDER

Guessing and checking helps you find reasonable guesses to solve a problem. For each guess, look at the important information. Check each guess against the information. Base the next guess on the previous result. (Was it too large or too small?) Recording your guesses and results in a table helps, too!

Work It Out

Guess	1	2	3	4	5	Guess	1	2	3	4	5
Number of Flamingos						Number of Flamingo Legs					
Number of Zebras						Number of Zebra Legs					

Write About It

What's the Problem?

A piano has 88 keys. There are 16 more white keys than black keys.

How many white keys does a piano have?

60

How many black keys does a piano have?

28

Use the table below if needed.

REMINDER

Guessing and checking helps you find reasonable guesses to solve a problem. For each guess, look at the important information. Check each guess against the information. Base the next guess on the previous result. (Was it too large or too small?) Recording your guesses and results in a table helps, too!

Work It Out

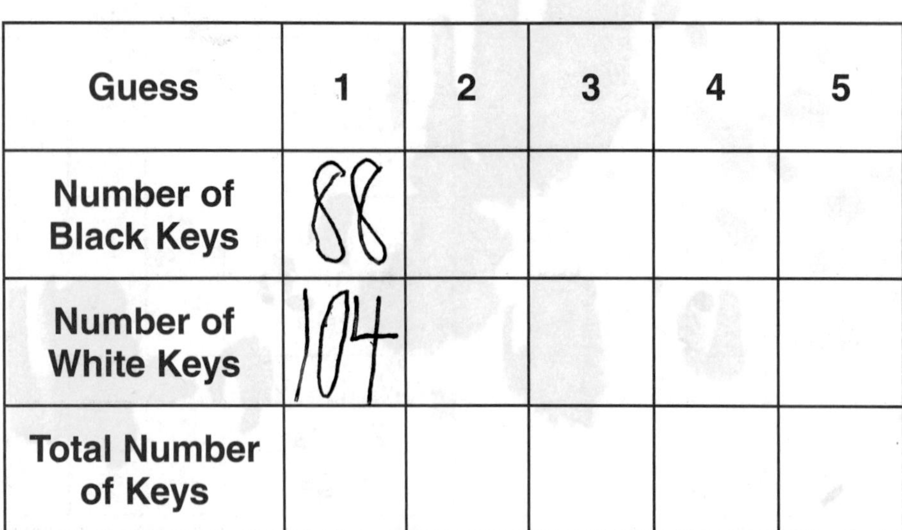

Guess	1	2	3	4	5
Number of Black Keys	88				
Number of White Keys	104				
Total Number of Keys					

Write About It

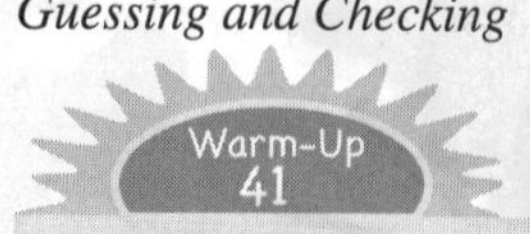

What's the Problem?

Lexi found 2 consecutive (in order) numbers that have a sum of 99.

What 2 numbers did Lexi find?

____

Use the table below if needed.

REMINDER

Guessing and checking helps you find reasonable guesses to solve a problem. For each guess, look at the important information. Check each guess against the information. Base the next guess on the previous result. (Was it too large or too small?) Recording your guesses and results in a table helps, too!

Work It Out

Guess	1	2	3	4	5
Number #1					
Number #2					
Total of Numbers					

Write About It

What's the Problem?

Using the numbers 0 to 8, place the numbers in the square so that each row and column has a sum of 12. (Each number can only be used 1 time.)

Complete the table below.

REMINDER

Guessing and checking helps you find reasonable guesses to solve a problem. For each guess, look at the important information. Check each guess against the information. Base the next guess on the previous result. (Was it too large or too small?) Recording your guesses and results in a table helps, too!

Work It Out

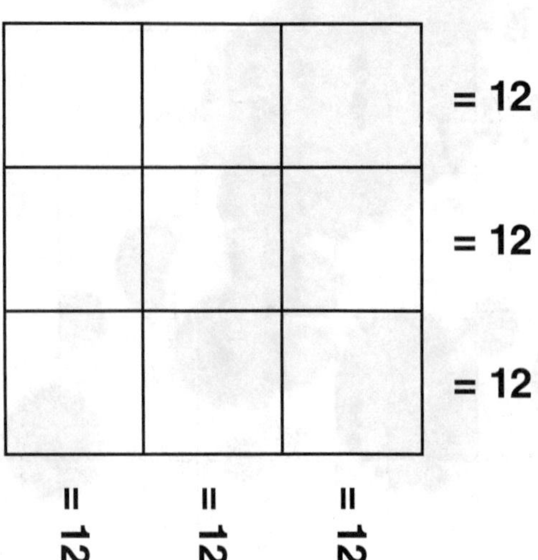

Write About It

What's the Problem?

Together, the cat and the dog weigh 90 pounds. The dog weighs twice as much as the cat.

How much does each animal weigh?

____

____

Use the table below if needed.

REMINDER

Guessing and checking helps you find reasonable guesses to solve a problem. For each guess, look at the important information. Check each guess against the information. Base the next guess on the previous result. (Was it too large or too small?) Recording your guesses and results in a table helps, too!

Work It Out

Guess	1	2	3	4	5	6	7	8
Weight of Dog								
Weight of Cat								
Total Weight								

Write About It

What's the Problem?

Gavin counted starfish and octopuses. There were 2 more octopuses than starfish. There were 14 animals in all.

How many octopuses were there? ____________

How many starfish were there?

____

Use the table below if needed.

> **REMINDER**
>
> Guessing and checking helps you find reasonable guesses to solve a problem. For each guess, look at the important information. Check each guess against the information. Base the next guess on the previous result. (Was it too large or too small?) Recording your guesses and results in a table helps, too!

Work It Out

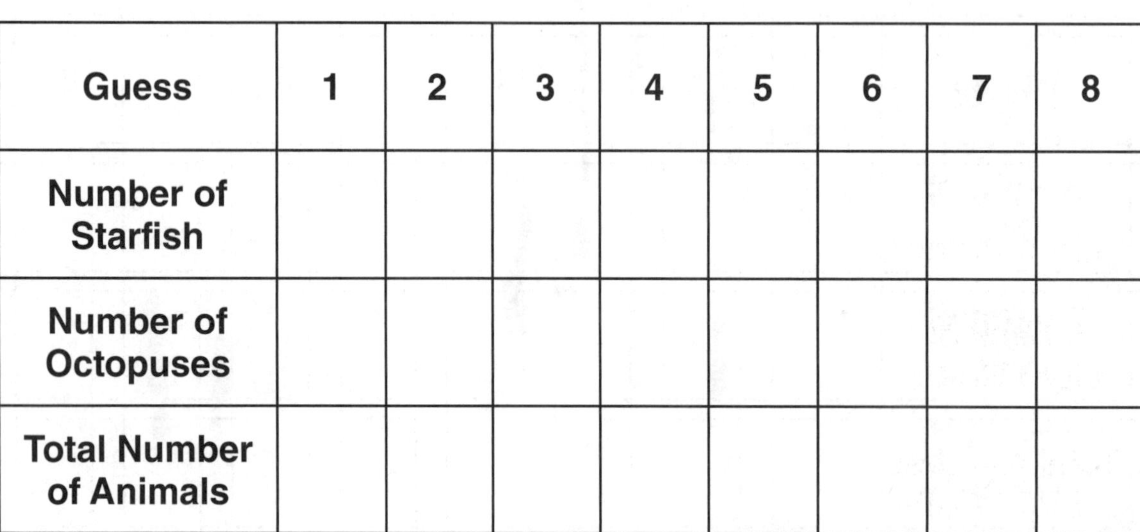

Guess	1	2	3	4	5	6	7	8
Number of Starfish								
Number of Octopuses								
Total Number of Animals								

Write About It

What's the Problem?

The Hardware Store sells light bulbs in packs of 4 or 5.

What is the fewest number of packs of light bulbs Melanie can buy to have exactly 33 light bulbs?

____

Use the table below if needed.

REMINDER

Guessing and checking helps you find reasonable guesses to solve a problem. For each guess, look at the important information. Check each guess against the information. Base the next guess on the previous result. (Was it too large or too small?) Recording your guesses and results in a table helps, too!

Work It Out

Guess	1	2	3	4	5	6	7	8
4-pack of Light Bulbs								
5-pack of Light Bulbs								
Total Number of Light Bulbs								

Write About It

What's the Problem?

Sarah has 5 coins worth 57 cents.

Which coins does Sarah have?

___

Use the table below if needed.

REMINDER

Guessing and checking helps you find reasonable guesses to solve a problem. For each guess, look at the important information. Check each guess against the information. Base the next guess on the previous result. (Was it too large or too small?) Recording your guesses and results in a table helps, too!

Work It Out

Guess	1	2	3	4	5	6	7	8
Penny								
Nickel								
Dime								
Quarter								
Total Number of Coins								
Total Amount								

Write About It

What's the Problem?

Heath picked 10 more cucumbers than squash. There were 20 vegetables picked in all.

How many of each kind of vegetable did Heath pick?

____

Use the table below if needed.

REMINDER

Guessing and checking helps you find reasonable guesses to solve a problem. For each guess, look at the important information. Check each guess against the information. Base the next guess on the previous result. (Was it too large or too small?) Recording your guesses and results in a table helps, too!

Work It Out

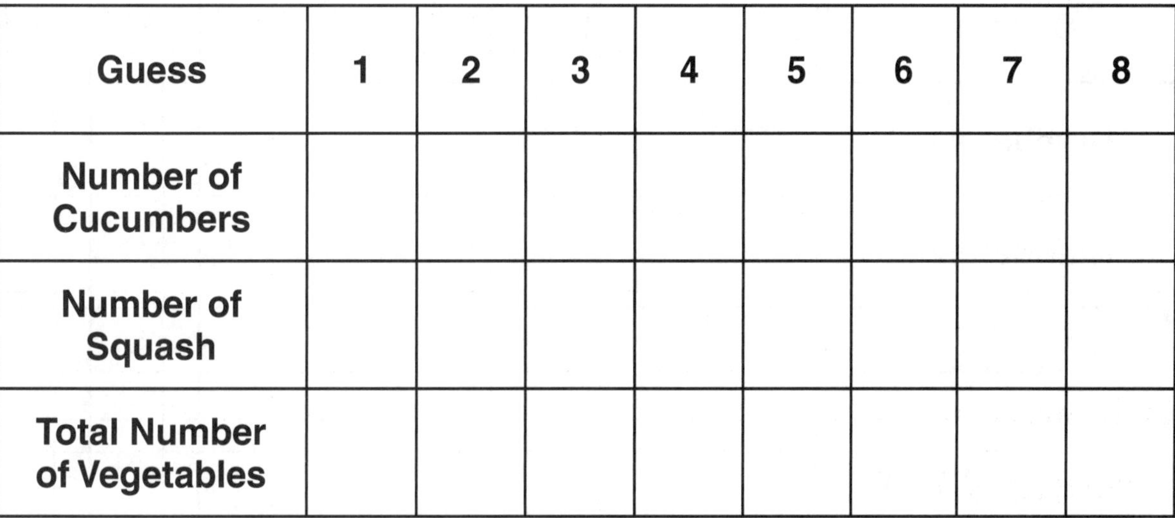

Guess	1	2	3	4	5	6	7	8
Number of Cucumbers								
Number of Squash								
Total Number of Vegetables								

Write About It

What's the Problem?

Ian skip counted by 2s. He found 3 numbers (in order) that when added together have a sum of 99.

Which 3 numbers did Ian find?

____

Use the table below if needed.

REMINDER

Guessing and checking helps you find reasonable guesses to solve a problem. For each guess, look at the important information. Check each guess against the information. Base the next guess on the previous result. (Was it too large or too small?) Recording your guesses and results in a table helps, too!

Work It Out

Guess	1	2	3	4	5	6	7	8
Number #1								
Number #2								
Number #3								
Total of Numbers								

Write About It

What's the Problem?

Karen drew a total of 8 shapes. Some were pentagons and some were triangles. Together, the total number of sides on the pentagons is the same as the total number of sides on the triangles.

How many of each shape did Karen draw?

____

Use the table below if needed.

REMINDER

Guessing and checking helps you find reasonable guesses to solve a problem. For each guess, look at the important information. Check each guess against the information. Base the next guess on the previous result. (Was it too large or too small?) Recording your guesses and results in a table helps, too!

Work It Out

Guess	1	2	3	4	5
Number of Pentagons					
Number of Triangles					
Total Number of Shapes					

Guess	1	2	3	4	5
Number of Sides–Pentagons					
Number of Sides–Triangles					

Write About It

What's the Problem?

Gabby placed numbers on the triangle so that each side had a sum of 20. She used the numbers 4 through 9. Each number was used one time.

How did Gabby arrange the numbers?

Use the diagram below if needed.

REMINDER

Guessing and checking helps you find reasonable guesses to solve a problem. For each guess, look at the important information. Check each guess against the information. Base the next guess on the previous result. (Was it too large or too small?) Recording your guesses and results in a table helps, too!

Work It Out

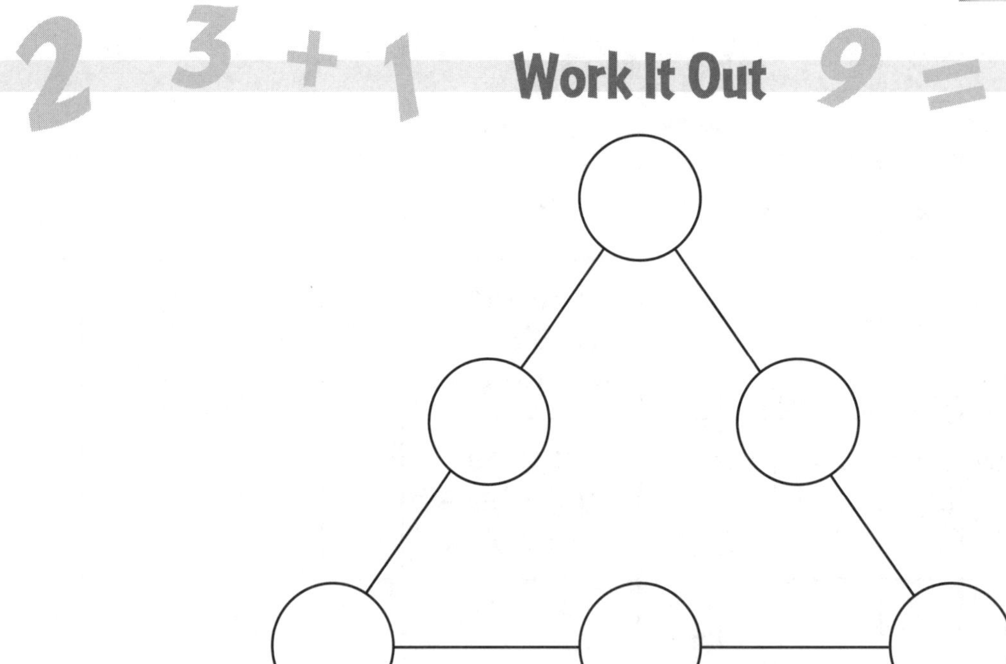

Write About It

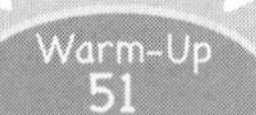

What's the Problem?

Work It Out

How many different 2-digit numbers can be made using the digits 1, 2, and 8?

____

Use each digit only once in each number.

WRITE ABOUT IT

____

____

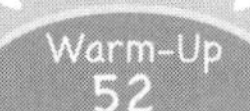

What's the Problem?

Work It Out

How many different 3-digit numbers can be made using the digits 1, 2, and 8?

____

Use each digit only once in each number.

WRITE ABOUT IT

____

____

What's the Problem?

Work It Out

There are 3 children in the Smith family. Jenny is 3 years old. Seth is twice as old as Jenny. Roger is 5 years older than Seth.

How old is each child in the Smith family?

WRITE ABOUT IT

Warm-Up 54

What's the Problem?

Work It Out

Roscoe and his twin brother, Jacob, are having a birthday party. They each invite 3 friends to the party.

How many people, including Roscoe and Jacob, will be at the party?

WRITE ABOUT IT

What's the Problem?

Work It Out

Travis planted 7 rows of tulips.
He planted 10 tulips in each row.

How many tulips did Travis plant in all?

____

WRITE ABOUT IT

____

____

What's the Problem?

Work It Out

Edwina brought juice to the party. There were 8 juice boxes in each package. Edwina brought 4 packages to the party.

How many juice boxes were there in all?

____

WRITE ABOUT IT

____

____

Warm-Up 57

What's the Problem?

Work It Out

Christopher had 32 pencils. He gave half of them to his brother, Julian. Out of his remaining pencils, Christopher gave half of them to his sister, Mary.

How many pencils does Christopher have left?

WRITE ABOUT IT

What's the Problem?

Work It Out

Bella had 20 newspapers. She delivered half to the homes on Elm Street. Out of the remaining newspapers, Bella delivered half to the homes on Pine Street. Bella then delivered 1 newspaper to her own home.

How many newspapers did Bella have left?

WRITE ABOUT IT

What's the Problem?

Name 4 different ways that the number 58 can be represented.

____

____

____

____

Work It Out

WRITE ABOUT IT

Warm-Up 60

What's the Problem?

Name 4 different ways that the number 139 can be represented.

____

____

____

____

Work It Out

WRITE ABOUT IT

Warm-Up 61

What's the Problem?

Work It Out

Hunter and Monty ordered an 8-slice pizza. Hunter ate half the pizza. Monty ate 2 slices of pizza.

Who ate more pizza?

____

WRITE ABOUT IT

Warm-Up 62

What's the Problem?

Work It Out

The scouts made 1 dozen cupcakes. Half of the cupcakes were chocolate, $\frac{1}{3}$ were vanilla, and the rest were strawberry.

How many cupcakes of each flavor did the scouts make?

____

____

WRITE ABOUT IT

What's the Problem?

Work It Out

Sue was working on a 300-piece puzzle. She put 175 of the pieces together.

How many pieces does Sue have left?

____

WRITE ABOUT IT

____

____

Warm-Up 64

What's the Problem?

Work It Out

Dax was trying to empty the gumballs from the gumball machine into the box. While pouring the 400 gumballs from the machine, 129 fell on the floor.

How many gumballs landed in the box?

____

WRITE ABOUT IT

____

____

What's the Problem?

Work It Out

Sam drew place value blocks to show the number 62. This is what Sam drew:

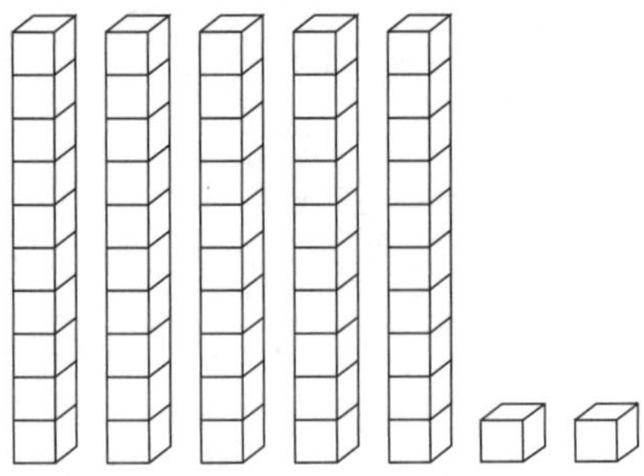

Is Sam correct? Why?

WRITE ABOUT IT

Warm-Up 66

What's the Problem?

Work It Out

Marisa drew place value blocks to show the number 207.

What did she draw?

WRITE ABOUT IT

Warm-Up 67

What's the Problem?

Work It Out

Use the digits 4, 6, and 8 to make four different 2-digit numbers.

Use each digit only once in each number.

Order the numbers from least to greatest.

____

____

____

____

WRITE ABOUT IT

Warm-Up 68

What's the Problem?

Work It Out

Use the digits 1, 3, 5, and 7 to make four different 3-digit numbers.

Use each digit only once in each number.

Order the numbers from greatest to least.

____

____

____

____

WRITE ABOUT IT

Warm-Up 69

What's the Problem?

Work It Out

Use the numbers 8, 9, and 17 to make two addition problems and two subtraction problems.

____

____

____

____

WRITE ABOUT IT

Warm-Up 70

What's the Problem?

Work It Out

Use the numbers 6, 14, and 20 to make two addition problems and two subtraction problems.

____

____

____

____

WRITE ABOUT IT

What's the Problem?

Work It Out

Jack had 143 red candles and 429 blue candles.

What is the difference between the number of blue candles and red candles?

____

WRITE ABOUT IT

____

____

What's the Problem?

Work It Out

Petra picked 248 peaches and 506 plums.

How many more plums than peaches did Petra pick?

____

WRITE ABOUT IT

____

____

Warm-Up 73

What's the Problem?

Work It Out

Neela made 5 rows of candy. She put 8 pieces of candy in each row.

How many pieces of candy does Neela have in all?

____

WRITE ABOUT IT

____

____

Warm-Up 74

What's the Problem?

Work It Out

Osbaldo arranged hats in 6 rows. He put 3 hats in each row.

How many hats does Osbaldo have in all?

____

WRITE ABOUT IT

____

____

What's the Problem?

Work It Out

Judy made 27 bows. She shared them equally among 3 friends.

How many bows did each friend get?

____

WRITE ABOUT IT

____

____

Warm-Up 76

What's the Problem?

Work It Out

Abner had a can filled with 40 olives. He divided the olives equally among 10 sandwiches.

How many olives were on each sandwich?

____

WRITE ABOUT IT

____

____

Warm-Up 77

What's the Problem?

Work It Out

How many multiplication problems can be made using two of the following numbers: 1, 2 and 5? ___________

What are they?

Use each number only once in each problem.

WRITE ABOUT IT

____

____

Warm-Up 78

What's the Problem?

Work It Out

How many multiplication problems can be made using two of the following numbers: 1, 2, 5, and 10? _______

What are they?

Use each number only once in each problem.

WRITE ABOUT IT

____

____

What's the Problem?

Work It Out

Jennifer had 12 bracelets. She gave half of them to a friend.

How many bracelets does Jennifer have left?

____

WRITE ABOUT IT

____

____

Warm-Up 80

What's the Problem?

Work It Out

Louis had 12 marbles. He gave $\frac{1}{3}$ of them to his brother.

How many marbles does Louis have left?

____

WRITE ABOUT IT

____

____

Warm-Up 81

What's the Problem?

Work It Out

Max ordered 3 pizzas. Each pizza was cut into 4 slices. Max ate $1\frac{1}{2}$ pizzas.

How many slices did Max eat?

____

WRITE ABOUT IT

Warm-Up 82

What's the Problem?

Work It Out

Jamie baked 4 pies. Each pie was cut into 6 pieces. Jamie sold $2\frac{1}{2}$ pies.

How many pieces did Jamie sell in all?

____

WRITE ABOUT IT

Warm-Up 83

What's the Problem?

Work It Out

Dolly had 87 cents. She gave her sister 34 cents.

How much money does Dolly have left?

____

WRITE ABOUT IT

Warm-Up 84

What's the Problem?

Work It Out

Dale had 93 cents. He bought a toy for 62 cents.

How much money does Dale have left?

____

WRITE ABOUT IT

What's the Problem?

Work It Out

There were 76 pencils in the box. The teacher used 24 pencils.

How many pencils are left?

____

WRITE ABOUT IT

____

____

What's the Problem?

Work It Out

Jeb had 145 stamps. He used 112 stamps to mail a package.

How many stamps does Jeb have left?

____

WRITE ABOUT IT

____

____

Warm-Up 87

What's the Problem?

Work It Out

Michael pulled some coins from his pocket. He had 1 half-dollar, 3 pennies, 1 quarter, 2 nickels, and 1 dime.

How much money did Michael have?

____

WRITE ABOUT IT

____

____

Warm-Up 88

What's the Problem?

Work It Out

Julie emptied her piggy bank. She had 3 quarters, 4 pennies, 1 dime, and 1 nickel.

How much money was in Julie's piggy bank?

____

WRITE ABOUT IT

____

____

Warm-Up 89

What's the Problem?

Which is more money —
3 quarters or 6 dimes? Why?

Work It Out

WRITE ABOUT IT

Warm-Up 90

What's the Problem?

Which is more money —
2 half-dollars or
100 pennies? Why?

Work It Out

WRITE ABOUT IT

Warm-Up 91

What's the Problem?

Work It Out

One triangle has 3 sides and 3 corners.

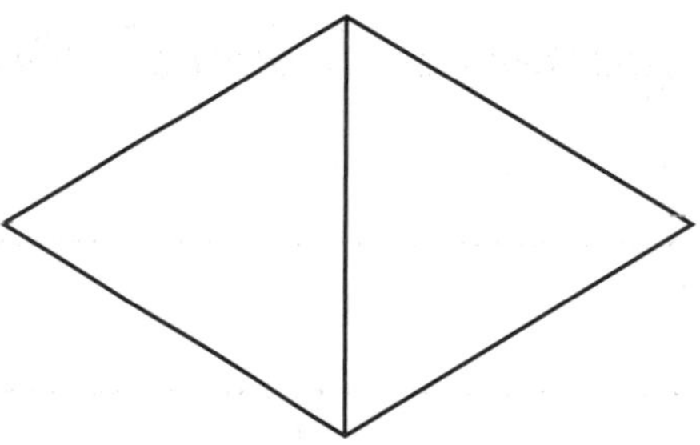

If 2 triangles are put together so that their sides are touching, how many sides and corners will there be?

____

Use the picture to help you.

WRITE ABOUT IT

____

____

Warm-Up 92

What's the Problem?

Work It Out

One trapezoid has 4 sides and 4 corners.

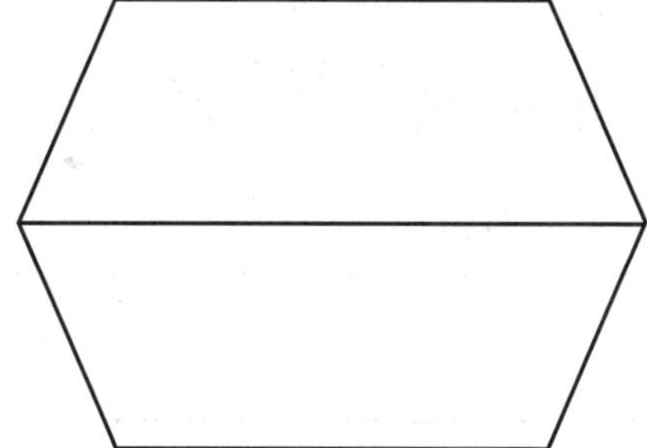

If one trapezoid is put above another trapezoid, how many sides and corners will there be?

____

Use the picture to help you.

WRITE ABOUT IT

____

____

Warm-Up 93

What's the Problem?

Work It Out

Lacy divided a square in half.

What shapes could she have made?

Draw them.

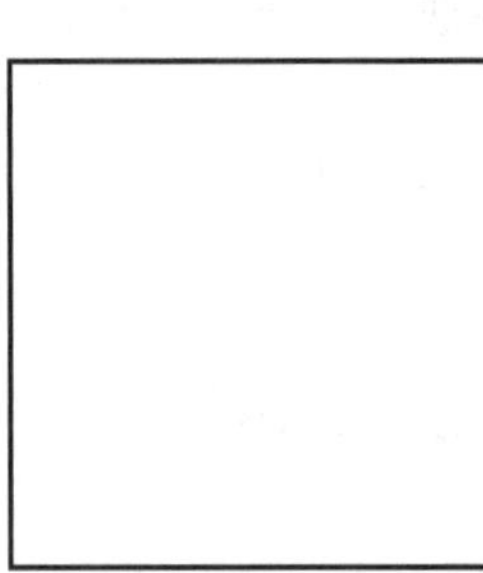

WRITE ABOUT IT

Warm-Up 94

What's the Problem?

Work It Out

Travis divided a rectangle into 3 equal parts.

What shapes could Travis have made?

Draw them.

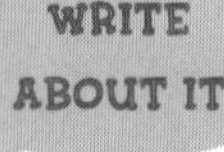

WRITE ABOUT IT

Warm-Up 95

What's the Problem?

Work It Out

How many different 4-sided shapes can you draw?

____

How are they alike?

____

How are they different?

____

WRITE ABOUT IT

Warm-Up 96

What's the Problem?

Work It Out

How many different 5-sided shapes can you draw?

____

How are they alike?

____

How are they different?

____

WRITE ABOUT IT

Warm-Up 97

What's the Problem?

Work It Out

Ulysses put 2 squares together so that 2 sides touch.

What shape did he draw?

____

____

____

Warm-Up 98

What's the Problem?

Work It Out

Lucy put 2 triangles and 1 square together. She drew a 4-sided shape. Then she moved 1 of the triangles and drew a 3-sided shape.

What 2 shapes did Lucy make?

____

WRITE ABOUT IT

____

____

Warm-Up 99

What's the Problem?

Work It Out

Look at the cube on this page.

Label each part of the cube.

How many faces does it have?

____

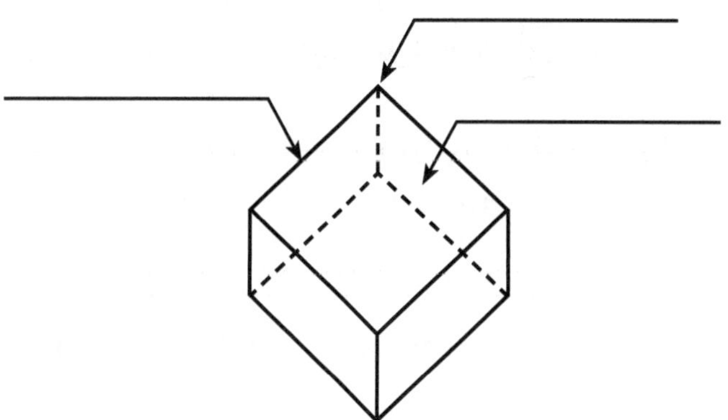

WRITE ABOUT IT

Warm-Up 100

What's the Problem?

Work It Out

How is a vertex (corner) of a shape different from an edge of a shape?

____

How many vertexes are on a cube?

____

How many edges are on a cube?

____

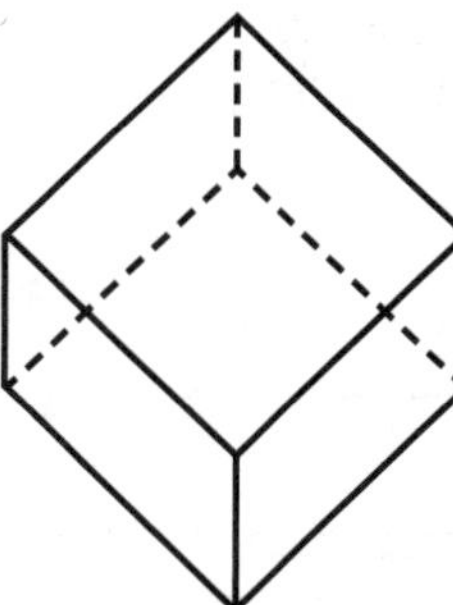

WRITE ABOUT IT

Warm-Up 101

What's the Problem?

Work It Out

Faith has a map of a local amusement park.

1. What is north of the Picnic Area?

____

2. What is east of the Bumper Cars?

____

3. What is west of the Snack Bar?

____

WRITE ABOUT IT

____

____

Warm-Up 102

What's the Problem?

Work It Out

Draw a map of the room you are in.

Mark your location with an X.

What items are to the north, east, south, and west of you?

____

____

WRITE ABOUT IT

____

____

Warm-Up 103

What's the Problem?

Write the location of each shape.

1. ☺ _____
2. ★ _____
3. ● _____
4. ☼ _____
5. ✿ _____
6. ♥ _____
7. ☾ _____
8. ▲ _____

Work It Out

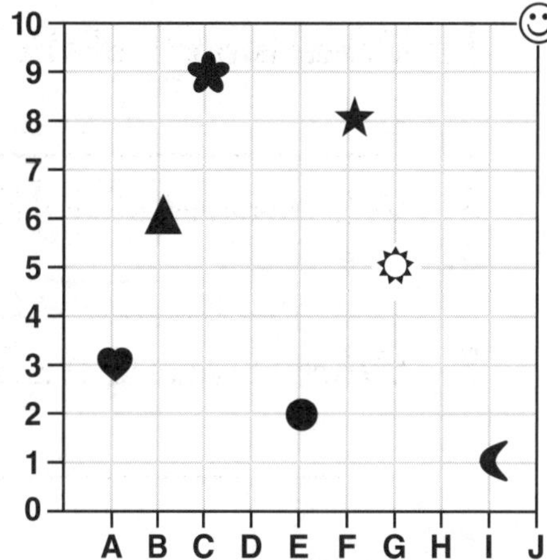

WRITE ABOUT IT

Warm-Up 104

What's the Problem?

Draw each shape on the coordinate grid.

1. ● A 6
2. ■ E 3
3. ▲ H 8
4. ⏢ C 10
5. ⬣ I 7
6. ⬟ G 1
7. ♥ B 4
8. ☾ F 9

Work It Out

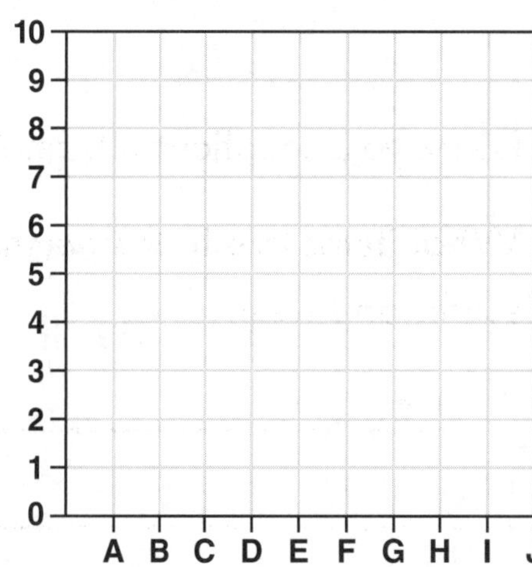

WRITE ABOUT IT

Warm-Up 105

What's the Problem?

Work It Out

Where is each item located?

1. The lamp is ______________ the sofa.
2. The cat is ______________ the sofa.
3. The dog is______________ the sofa.
4. The table is ______________ the sofa.

WRITE ABOUT IT

Warm-Up 106

What's the Problem?

Work It Out

Draw the picture described below.

- Draw a tree.
- Draw an apple under the tree.
- Draw a bird in the tree.
- Draw a sun above the tree.
- Draw a swing next to the tree.

WRITE ABOUT IT

What's the Problem?

Work It Out

How are a square and a cube alike?

____

How are they different?

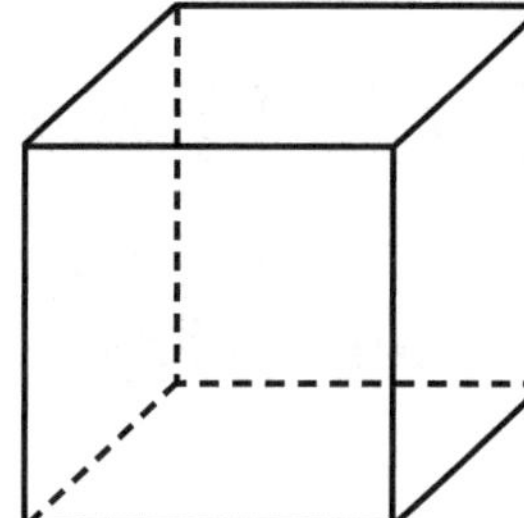

____

WRITE ABOUT IT

____

____

Warm-Up 108

What's the Problem?

Work It Out

How are a triangle and a triangular pyramid alike?

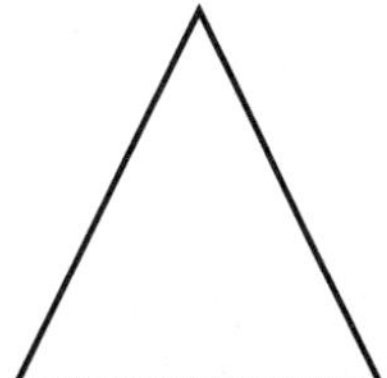

____

How are they different?

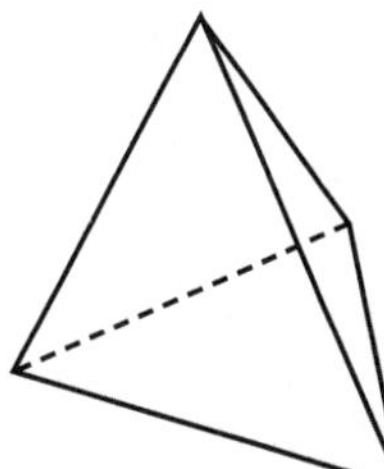

____

WRITE ABOUT IT

____

____

Warm-Up 109

What's the Problem?

Work It Out

Erin's dad wanted to paint a set of 10 wooden cubes for Erin's room. He will paint 4 cubes red and 6 cubes yellow.

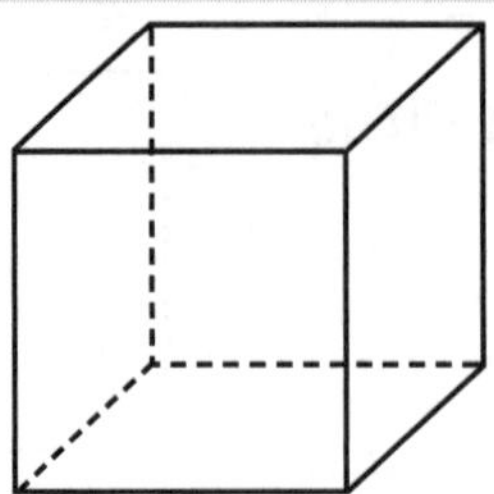

How many cube faces will he paint red?

____

How many cube faces will he paint yellow?

____

WRITE ABOUT IT

Warm-Up 110

What's the Problem?

Work It Out

Ralph needed to make 5 triangular pyramids to hang for a party decoration. On each face, he wanted to add a friend's name.

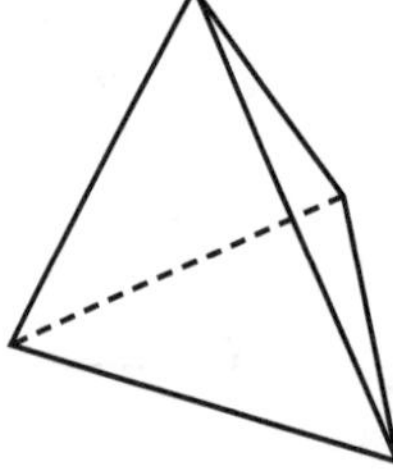

How many names can he write on the pyramids altogether?

____

WRITE ABOUT IT

What's the Problem?

Work It Out

Jamie drew 2 shapes on the chalkboard.

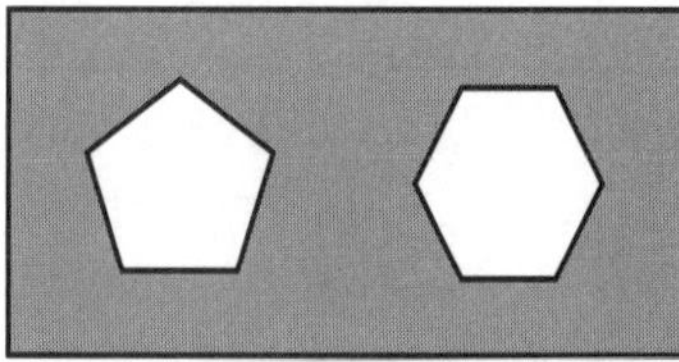

What shapes did she draw?

____

WRITE ABOUT IT

____

____

Warm-Up 112

What's the Problem?

Work It Out

Max drew 2 shapes on the chalkboard.

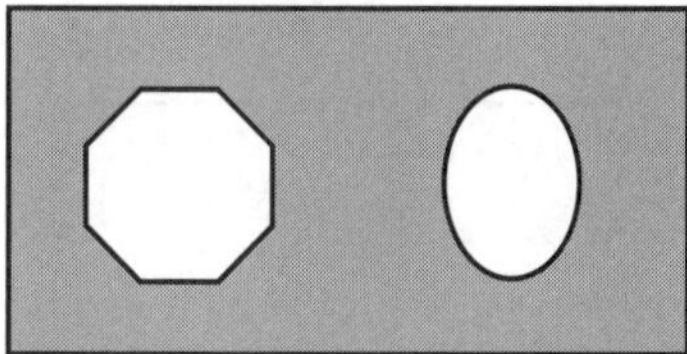

What shapes did he draw?

____

WRITE ABOUT IT

____

____

Warm-Up 113

What's the Problem?

Tawny had a trapezoid. She transformed (changed) the shape by sliding, flipping, and turning it.

Draw the trapezoid after each transformation.

Use arrows to show how the shape changed.

Work It Out

Sliding Flipping Turning

WRITE ABOUT IT

Warm-Up 114

What's the Problem?

Tristan had a pentagon. He transformed (changed) the shape by sliding, flipping, and turning it.

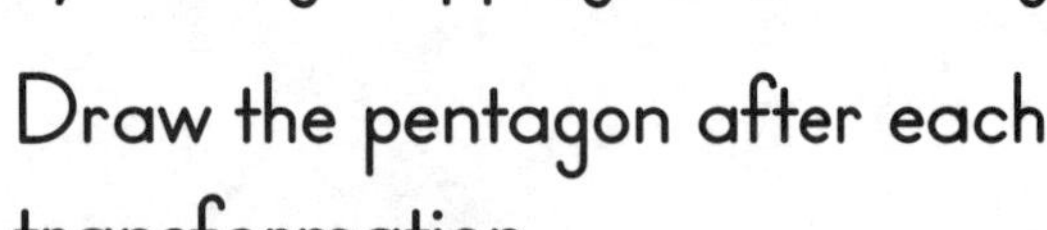

Draw the pentagon after each transformation.

Use arrows to show how the shape changed.

Work It Out

Sliding Flipping Turning

WRITE ABOUT IT

What's the Problem?

Work It Out

Betty looked around the room and noticed a lot of things were shaped like cubes.

What kinds of things could Betty have seen?

Draw and label the items.

WRITE ABOUT IT

Warm-Up 116

What's the Problem?

Work It Out

Fred was at a local store. He saw many things shaped like spheres.

What kinds of things could Fred have seen?

Draw and label the items.

WRITE ABOUT IT

Warm-Up 117

What's the Problem?

Amanda drew a triangle.

Draw another triangle that is congruent to Amanda's triangle.

Work It Out

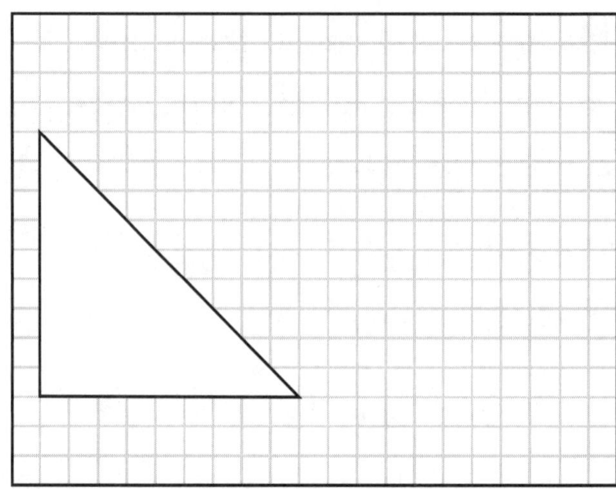

WRITE ABOUT IT

Warm-Up 118

What's the Problem?

Ben drew a trapezoid.

Draw another trapezoid that is congruent to Ben's trapezoid.

Work It Out

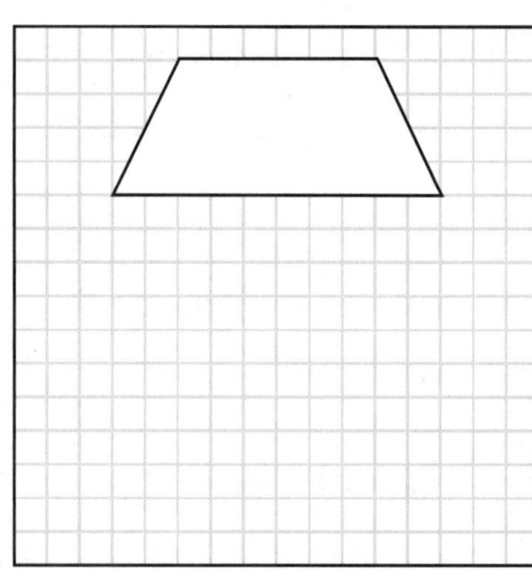

WRITE ABOUT IT

Warm-Up 119

What's the Problem?

Work It Out

Sort the solid shapes into 2 different groups.

How did you sort the solid shapes?

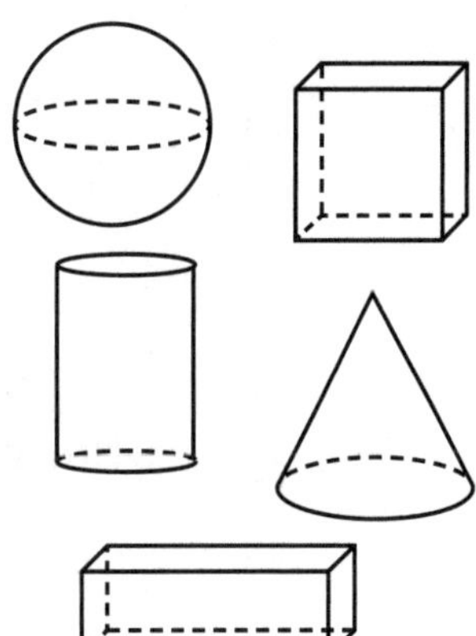

____

____

WRITE ABOUT IT

Warm-Up 120

What's the Problem?

Work It Out

Which solid shapes can be stacked?

____

Which solid shapes can roll?

____

Which solid shapes can be stacked and rolled?

____

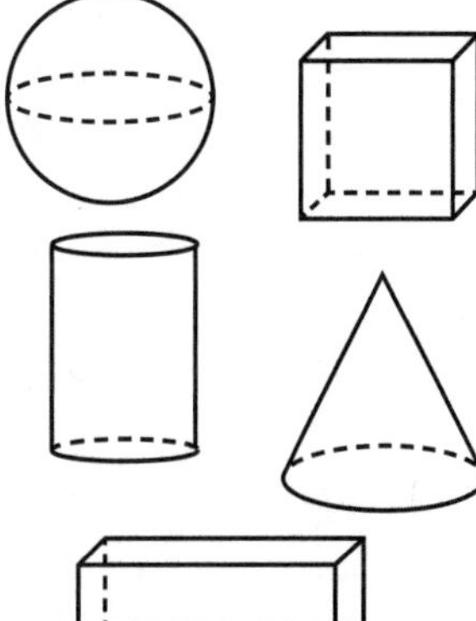

WRITE ABOUT IT

Warm-Up 121

What's the Problem?

Work It Out

Sara, Charles, and Tony all drew shapes on the board.

Who drew a shape with the most sides?

____

What is the name of the shape?

____

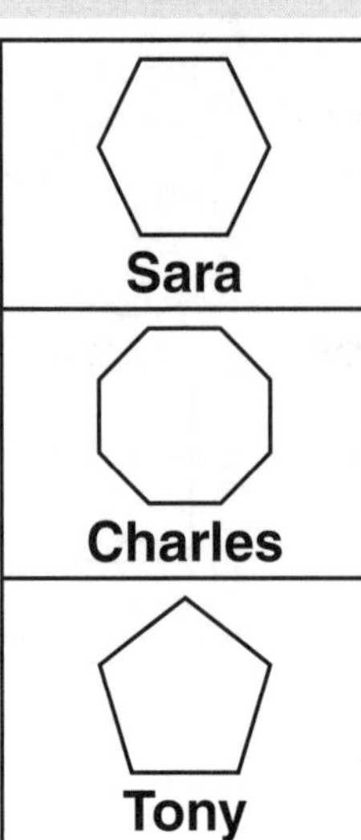

WRITE ABOUT IT

____

____

Warm-Up 122

What's the Problem?

Work It Out

Amethyst put a cylinder on a sheet of paper. She drew around the bottom of the cylinder.

What shape did she make on the paper?

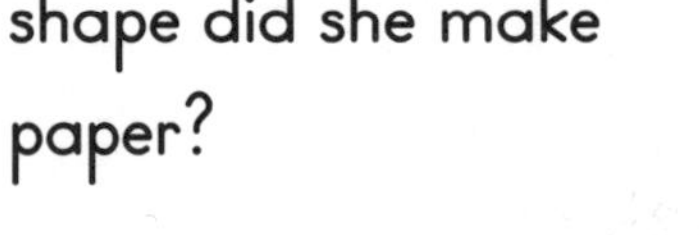

____

WRITE ABOUT IT

____

____

Warm-Up 123

What's the Problem?

Draw a shape or design on the grid.

Write the coordinates for each point on the design.

Work It Out

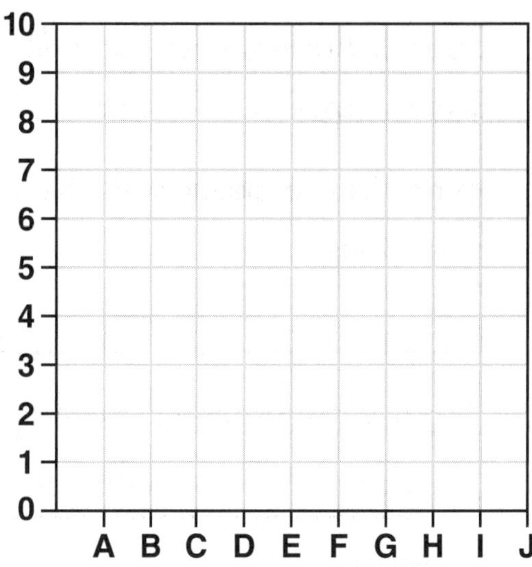

WRITE ABOUT IT

Warm-Up 124

What's the Problem?

Draw your favorite letter on the grid.

Write the coordinates for each point on the letter.

Work It Out

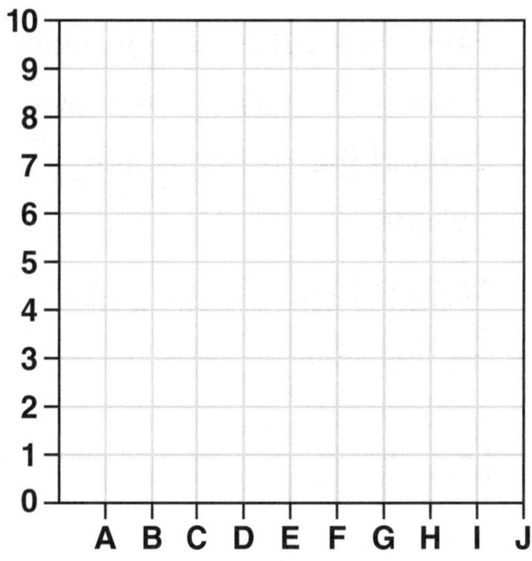

WRITE ABOUT IT

Warm-Up 125

What's the Problem?

Work It Out

Dan drew a square with sides of 5 pegs each.

What is the perimeter of the square?

____

What is the area of the square?

____

Use the picture to help you.

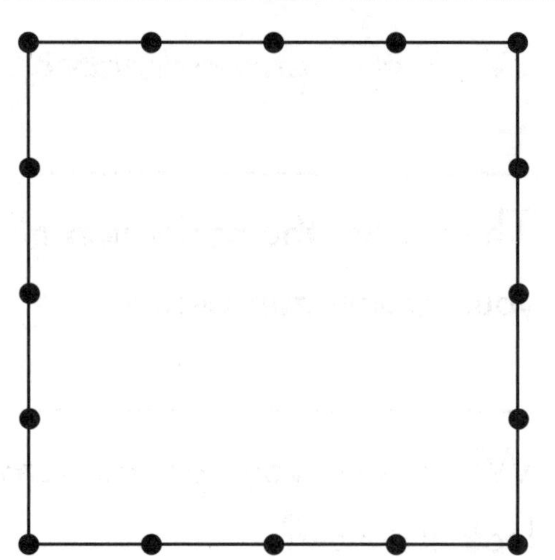

WRITE ABOUT IT

____

____

Warm-Up 126

What's the Problem?

Work It Out

Pam drew a rectangle with sides of 3 pegs and 7 pegs.

What is the perimeter of the rectangle?

____

What is the area of the rectangle?

____

Use the picture to help you.

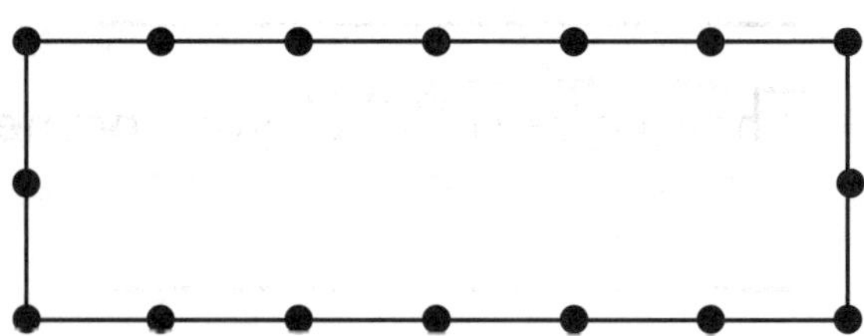

WRITE ABOUT IT

____

____

What's the Problem?

Work It Out

Write your phone number.

____

Then write the reflection of your phone number.

____

What does your phone number look like now?

WRITE ABOUT IT

____

____

Warm-Up 128

What's the Problem?

Work It Out

Write your name.

____

Then write a flip of your name.

____

What does your name look like now?

WRITE ABOUT IT

____

____

Warm-Up 129

What's the Problem?

Work It Out

Vi drew several plane shapes.

- She drew a circle.
- She drew a star inside the circle.
- She drew a triangle to the right of the circle.
- Below the circle, Vi drew a heart.

What does Vi's drawing look like?

WRITE ABOUT IT

Warm-Up 130

What's the Problem?

Work It Out

Ryan drew several plane shapes.

- Ryan drew a square.
- He drew 2 lines to divide the square into 4 triangles.
- He drew another square on top of the first square.
- He divided the second square into 4 squares.

What does Ryan's drawing look like?

WRITE ABOUT IT

What's the Problem?

Work It Out

A carrot grows 1 inch every 3 days.

How many inches will the carrot grow in 1 week and 2 days?

____

WRITE ABOUT IT

____

____

Warm-Up 132

What's the Problem?

Work It Out

Steve has a board that is 1 foot long.

If he draws a line after each inch, how many lines will Steve draw?

____

WRITE ABOUT IT

____

____

Warm-Up 133

What's the Problem?

Work It Out

The Speedy Train leaves at 8:15 a.m. It arrives at its first stop at 8:45 a.m.

How many minutes does it take the train to reach the first stop?

____

WRITE ABOUT IT

Warm-Up 134

What's the Problem?

Work It Out

Mick rode his bicycle to school. It took him 10 minutes to get to school.

If Mick arrived at school at 8:30 a.m., what time did he leave his house?

____

WRITE ABOUT IT

What's the Problem?

Work It Out

Dana sleeps 8 hours each night.

If he has to get up at 7:00 a.m., what time should he go to bed?

____

WRITE ABOUT IT

___

___

Warm-Up 136

What's the Problem?

Work It Out

Diana catches the school bus at 7:45 a.m. It takes 50 minutes to ride to school.

What time does Diana arrive at school?

____

WRITE ABOUT IT

___

___

What's the Problem?

Work It Out

Jeremy had a bat that was 1 foot long.

How many inches long was the bat?

____

WRITE ABOUT IT

____

____

Warm-Up 138

What's the Problem?

Work It Out

Kelly's footsteps are 3 feet apart.

How many inches are in 3 feet?

____

WRITE ABOUT IT

____

____

Warm-Up 139

What's the Problem?

The school year ends on June 10 and begins again on August 16.

How many days of summer vacation will the students have? Use the calendar to help you.

____

Note: There are 30 days in June and 31 days in July and August.

Work It Out

June

S	M	T	W	Th	F	Sa
			1	2	3	4
5	6	7	8	9	10	11
12	13	14	15	16	17	18
19	20	21	22	23	24	25
26	27	28	29	30		

WRITE ABOUT IT

____

____

Warm-Up 140

What's the Problem?

Each year, many people celebrate Thanksgiving. It is always held on the fourth Thursday in November.

What is the date of Thanksgiving? Use the calendar to help you.

____

Work It Out

November

S	M	T	W	Th	F	Sa
	1	2	3	4	5	6
7	8	9	10	11	12	13
14	15	16	17	18	19	20
21	22	23	24	25	26	27
28	29	30				

WRITE ABOUT IT

____

____

What's the Problem?

Work It Out

At 8:00 a.m., the temperature was 50°F. By noon, the air had warmed up by 36°.

What was the temperature at 12:00 p.m.?

____

WRITE ABOUT IT

____

____

Warm-Up 142

What's the Problem?

Work It Out

At 4:00 p.m., the temperature was 75°F. During the night, the temperature dropped 34°.

What was the temperature that night?

____

WRITE ABOUT IT

____

____

What's the Problem?

Work It Out

Frito is 8 inches tall. Bandit is 4 inches taller than Frito, and Ranger is twice as tall as Frito.

How many inches tall are Bandit and Ranger?

____

____

WRITE ABOUT IT

Warm-Up 144

What's the Problem?

Work It Out

Homer the Rat's body is $1\frac{1}{2}$ inches long, and his tail is $\frac{1}{2}$ inch longer than his body.

How long is Homer's tail?

____

How long is Homer in all?

____

WRITE ABOUT IT

Warm-Up 145

What's the Problem?

Work It Out

Marco's hair grows $\frac{1}{2}$ inch per month.

How many inches will his hair grow in 3 months?

____

WRITE ABOUT IT

Warm-Up 146

What's the Problem?

Work It Out

Raquel had a 9-inch length of ribbon. She cut it into 3 pieces. The third piece is twice as long as the first and second pieces combined. The first piece is 1 inch long.

How long is each piece of ribbon?

WRITE ABOUT IT

What's the Problem?

Work It Out

Brenda measured her pillow.
The pillow was $1\frac{1}{2}$ feet long.

How many inches is that?

____

WRITE ABOUT IT

____

____

Warm-Up 148

What's the Problem?

Work It Out

Mark ate 2 foot-long hot dogs.

How many inches of hot dog
did Mark eat?

____

WRITE ABOUT IT

____

____

Warm-Up 149

What's the Problem?

Work It Out

Edith drew a line that was 8 inches long.

About how many centimeters long is the line?

Note: 1 inch = 2.54 centimeters

____

WRITE ABOUT IT

Warm-Up 150

What's the Problem?

Work It Out

Richard drew 2 lines. One line was 3 inches long. The other line was 3 centimeters long.

Which line was longer?

____

WRITE ABOUT IT

What's the Problem?

Work It Out

Tina wants to fill a pitcher with water.

Which measuring tool should she use: a ruler, a cup, or a thermometer? Why?

____

____

WRITE ABOUT IT

____

____

Warm-Up 152

What's the Problem?

Work It Out

David wants to weigh his pet rabbit.

Which measuring tool should he use: a scale, a ruler, or a cup? Why?

____

____

WRITE ABOUT IT

____

____

What's the Problem?

Work It Out

Glenda watched monkeys climb a tree. Glenda wants to measure how high in the tree the monkeys are.

What should she use to measure the tree? Why?

____

WRITE ABOUT IT

____

____

Warm-Up 154

What's the Problem?

Work It Out

Ricardo wants to measure the length of an ant.

Which would be the best measurement tool: a centimeter ruler or a scale? Why?

____

____

WRITE ABOUT IT

____

____

Warm-Up 155

What's the Problem?

Angel colored this shape.

What is the area of the shape Angel colored?

____

Work It Out

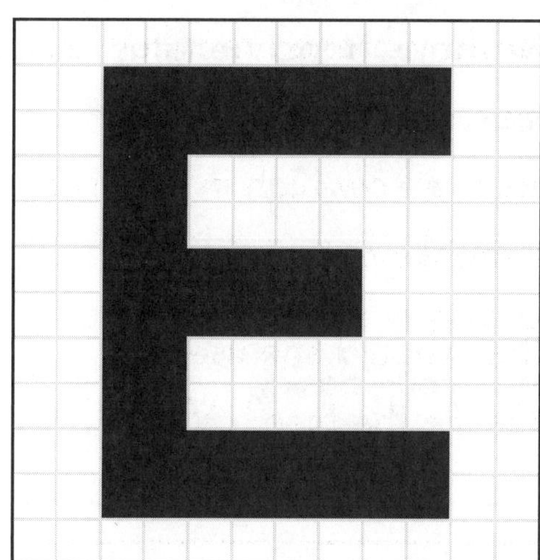

WRITE ABOUT IT

____

____

Warm-Up 156

What's the Problem?

Beth colored a shape with an area of 30 squares.

What could Beth's shape look like?

Work It Out

WRITE ABOUT IT

____

____

Warm-Up 157

What's the Problem?

How many hand-lengths wide is your desk?

____

How many hand-lengths long is your desk?

____

Work It Out

WRITE ABOUT IT

____

____

Warm-Up 158

What's the Problem?

How many crayons wide is your desk?

____

How many crayons long is your desk?

____

Work It Out

WRITE ABOUT IT

____

____

What's the Problem?

Work It Out

Tabitha measured the length of a dollar.

About how many inches long is a dollar bill?

____

WRITE ABOUT IT

____

____

Warm-Up 160

What's the Problem?

Work It Out

Using a dollar bill (or something the same length), measure the circumference of your head.

About how many dollar bills does it take to get around your head?

____

WRITE ABOUT IT

____

____

What's the Problem?

Work It Out

Ravi used a ruler to measure his pencil. His pencil was 9 inches long.

Is that more than 1 foot or less than 1 foot?

____

How do you know?

____

WRITE ABOUT IT

____

____

Warm-Up 162

What's the Problem?

Work It Out

Cut a piece of string or yarn that is the same height as you are.

How many inches long is the string?

____

Is it longer or shorter than 1 yard? How do you know?

____

WRITE ABOUT IT

____

____

What's the Problem?

Work It Out

Deb's mom picks her up at 3:00 p.m. It is now 2:55 p.m.

How much longer until Deb's mom picks her up?

____

WRITE ABOUT IT

____

____

Warm-Up 164

What's the Problem?

Work It Out

The school bus will arrive in 2 minutes.

How many seconds is that?

____

WRITE ABOUT IT

____

____

Warm-Up 165

What's the Problem?

Work It Out

The minute hand on a clock moved from the 1 to the 4.

How many minutes is that?

____

WRITE ABOUT IT

____

____

Warm-Up 166

What's the Problem?

Work It Out

The hour hand on a clock moved from the 6 to the 9.

How many hours is that?

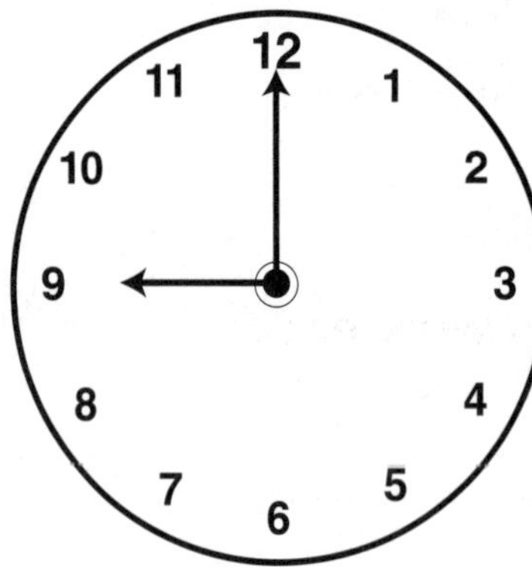

____

WRITE ABOUT IT

____

____

What's the Problem?

Work It Out

The television show is $\frac{1}{2}$ hour long. It ended at 7:30 a.m.

What time did the show start?

____

WRITE ABOUT IT

____

____

What's the Problem?

Work It Out

Mackie went for a 15-minute walk around the block. She began her walk at 4:15 p.m.

What time did Mackie's walk end?

____

WRITE ABOUT IT

____

____

What's the Problem?

Work It Out

Autumn and her family went camping for 2 weeks and 3 days.

How many days is that?

____

WRITE ABOUT IT

What's the Problem?

Work It Out

Matt's birthday is in 3 months.

About how many weeks is it until his birthday?

____

WRITE ABOUT IT

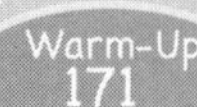

What's the Problem?

Aidan asked 10 people to name their favorite type of book. Two people picked mysteries, 3 people picked history, and 5 people picked animals.

Complete the chart using tally marks to show Aidan's information.

Favorite Book	Number of People
Mystery	
History	
Animals	

What's the Problem?

Matilda kept track of the type of bags students were using at school. Six students were using carrying backpacks, 7 students were using tote bags, and 8 students were using rolling backpacks.

Complete the chart using tally marks to show Matilda's information.

Type of Bag	Number of People
Carrying Backpack	
Tote Bag	
Rolling Backpack	

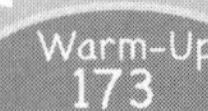

What's the Problem?

Mike asked 20 people if they used their left hand, right hand, or both hands for writing and playing sports. He made a chart showing their answers.

Left Hand	Both	Right Hand
6	2	12

Complete the Venn diagram to show Mike's findings. Use tally marks.

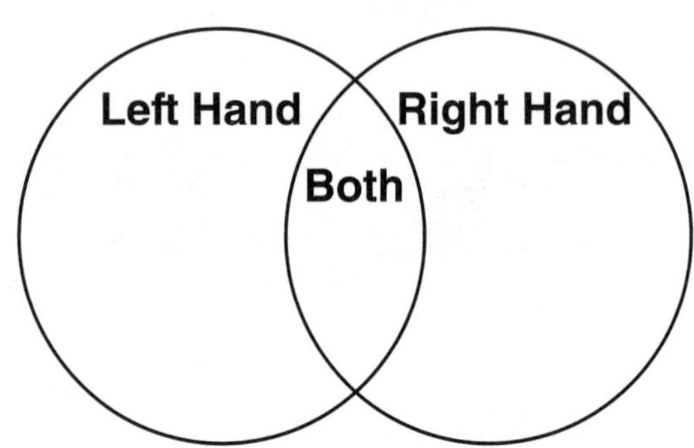

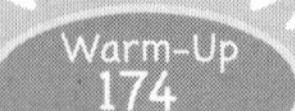

What's the Problem?

Gwen asked 20 people if they liked bats. She made a chart showing their answers.

Like Bats	Not Sure	Do Not Like Bats
11	1	8

Complete the Venn diagram to show Gwen's findings. Use tally marks.

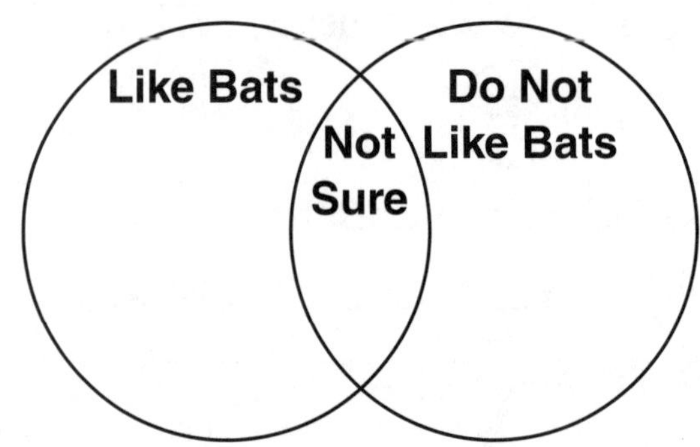

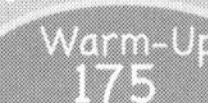

What's the Problem?

Miller asked 20 people which kind of phone they had. Miller made the following chart.

Make a bar graph showing Miller's data.

Type of Phone	Number of People
	𝍸 𝍸 𝍸
	𝍸

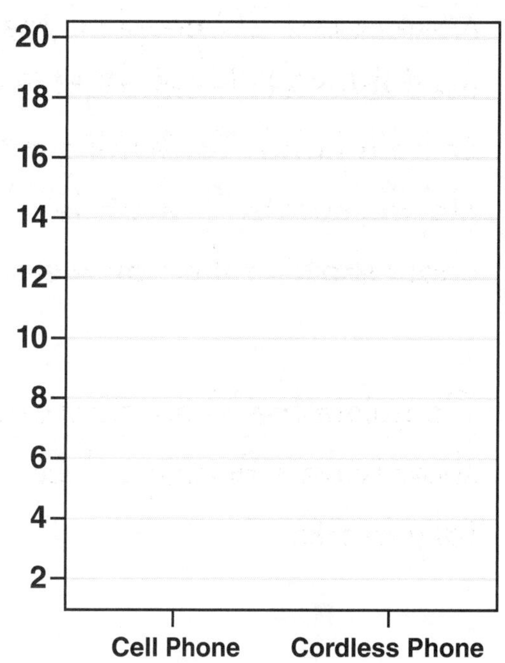

What's the Problem?

Shakira counted the type of lock 20 people used on their bikes. She made the following chart.

Make a bar graph showing Shakira's data.

Type of Lock	Number of People
	𝍸 𝍸
	𝍸 ||
	|||

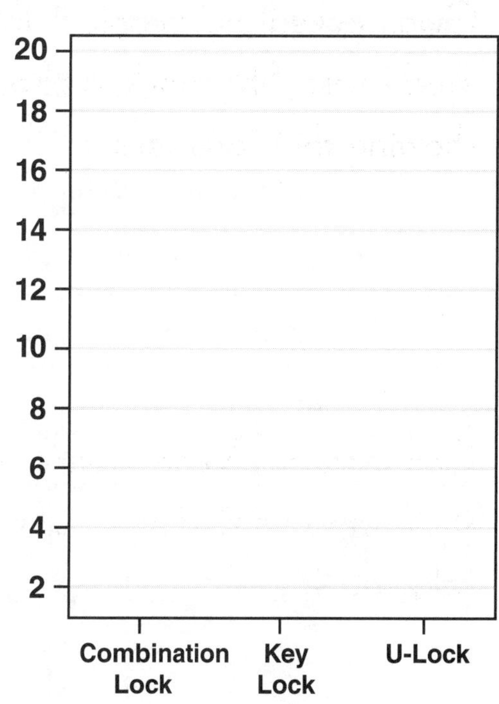

What's the Problem?

Ramon was taking inventory at Mateo's Game Store. He found and charted the following games: checkers, marbles, and jacks. Make a bar graph showing the games Ramon counted.

Type of Game	Number of Games
	卌
	卌
	|||

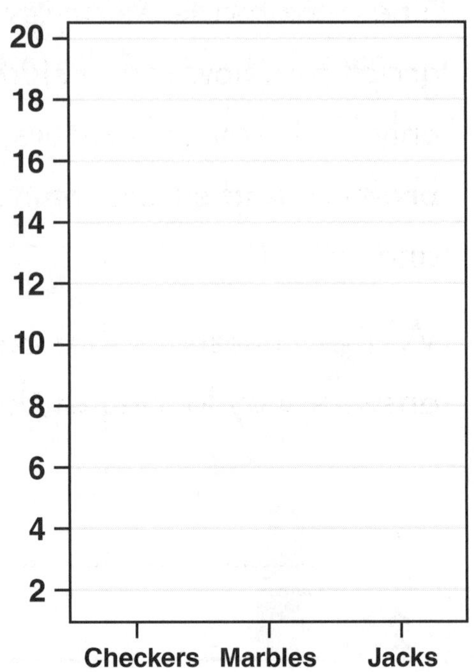

What's the Problem?

Berta was taking inventory at the Road Travel Shop. She counted and charted the following types of equipment: RVs, trailers, and tents. Make a bar graph showing the types of equipment Berta counted.

Type of Equipment	Number of Equipment
	卌 |
	|||
	|||

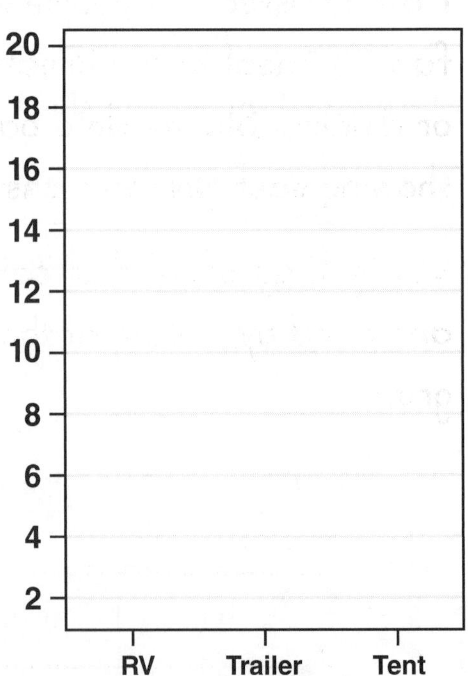

Warm-Up 179

What's the Problem?

The class made a bar graph. The graph tells how many students have only brothers, only sisters, both brothers and sisters, or no brothers and sisters.

Write 2 questions that can be answered by looking at the graph.

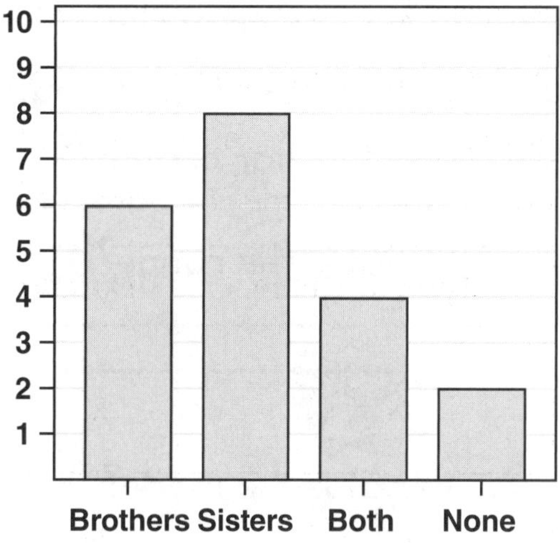

1. ______________________________

2. ______________________________

Warm-Up 180

What's the Problem?

Patrice asked 15 people what their favorite meal was—breakfast, lunch, or dinner. She made a bar graph showing each person's answer.

Write 2 questions that can be answered by looking at the graph.

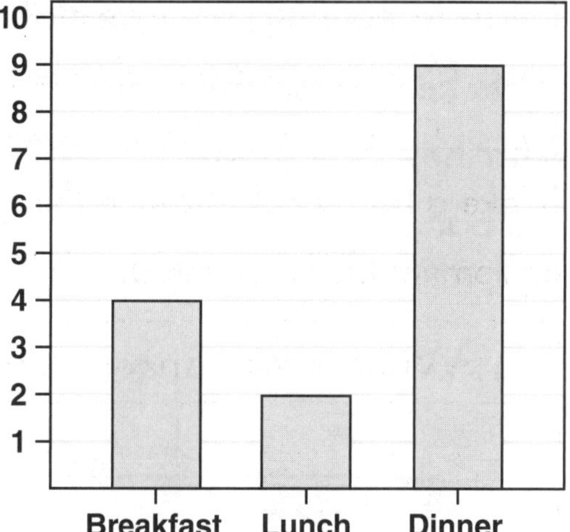

1. ______________________________

2. ______________________________

Warm-Up 181

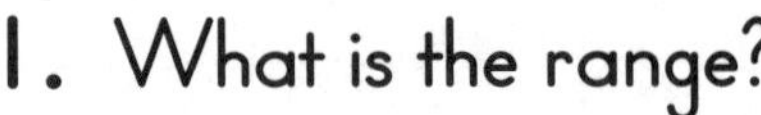

What's the Problem?

Roland kept track of the different flavors of gum sold. He made this bar graph.

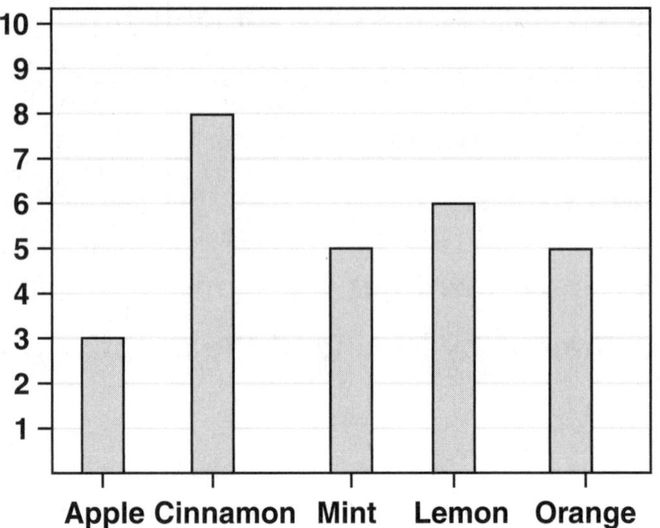

1. What is the range?

____

2. What is the mode?

____

Warm-Up 182

What's the Problem?

Yolanda counted the types of shirts her classmates were wearing. She made this bar graph.

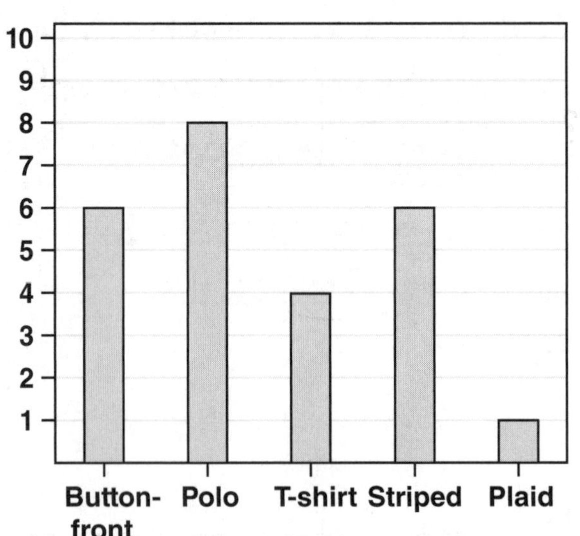

1. What is the range?

____

2. What is the mode?

____

What's the Problem?

Francine put 10 socks in a bag. Eight of the socks are red and the rest are blue.

1. Is it *likely* or *unlikely* that Francine will pull out a red sock?

   ____

2. Is it *likely* or *unlikely* that Francine will pull out a blue sock?

   ____

What's the Problem?

Trevor put 12 cards in a box. Three cards are face cards. The rest are numbered cards.

1. Is it *likely* or *unlikely* that Trevor will pull out a numbered card?

   ____

2. Is it *likely* or *unlikely* that Trevor will pull out a face card?

   ____

What's the Problem?

Trina made this spinner.

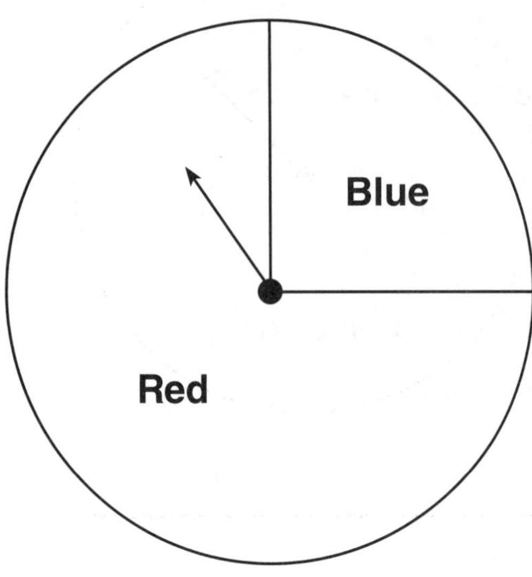

1. Is it *likely* or *unlikely* that the spinner will land on red? Why?

____

____

2. Is it *likely* or *unlikely* that the spinner will land on blue? Why?

____

____

What's the Problem?

Marvin made this spinner.

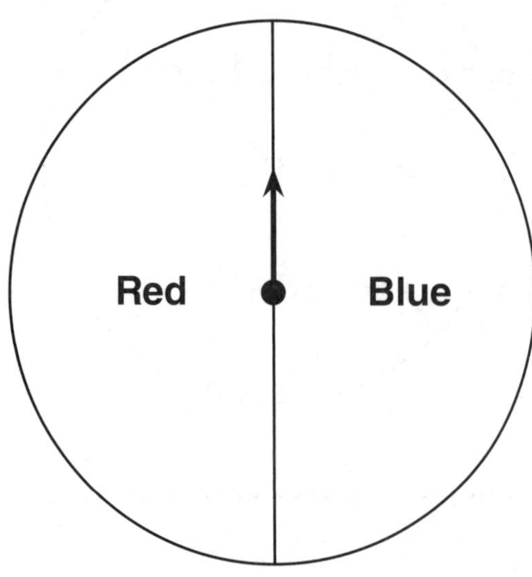

1. Is it *likely* or *unlikely* that the spinner will land on red? Why?

____

____

2. Is it *likely* or *unlikely* that the spinner will land on blue? Why?

____

____

What's the Problem?

Cyrus made a spinner. The spinner has 4 different colors on it. Cyrus made the spinner so that it has an equal chance of landing on each color.

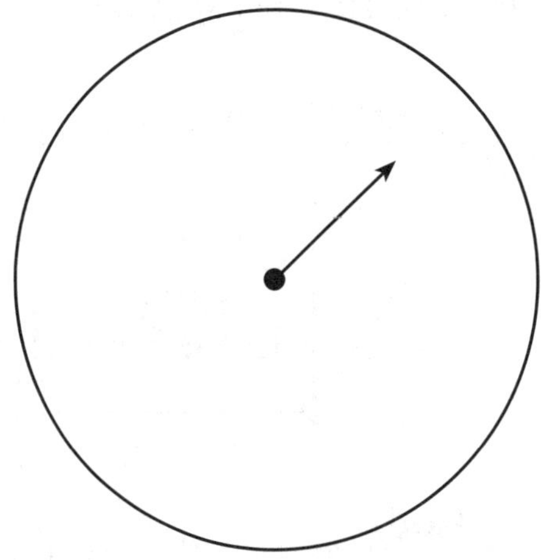

What does Cyrus's spinner look like?

Is it a fair spinner? Why or why not?

____

____

Warm-Up
188

What's the Problem?

Leslie made a spinner. The spinner has 4 different colors on it. Leslie made the spinner so that it has the greatest chance of landing on green.

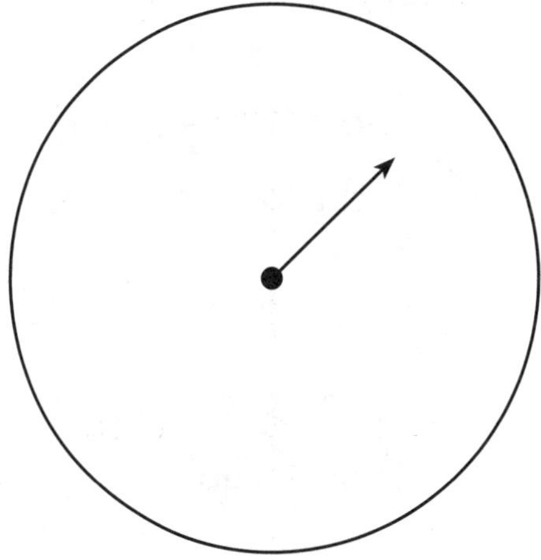

What does Leslie's spinner look like?

Is it a fair spinner? Why or why not?

____

____

What's the Problem?

Look at the graph.

1. Who ate the most pieces of pie? ______________

2. Who ate the fewest pieces of pie? ______________

3. What was the total number of pie slices eaten?

____

Person	Number of Slices Eaten
Adele	🥧 🥧 🥧
Brandy	🥧 🥧
Callie	🥧 🥧 🥧 🥧
🥧 = 2 slices of pie	

What's the Problem?

Look at the graph.

1. How many more cherries did Don eat than Fred?

____

2. Who ate fewer cherries than Fred?

____

3. How many cherries were eaten in all?

____

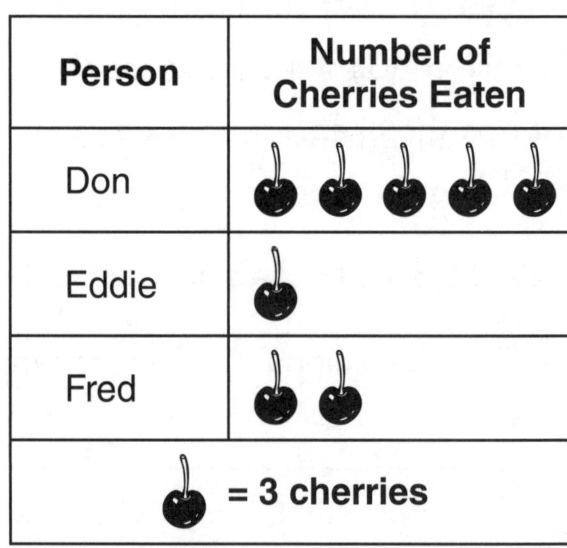

Person	Number of Cherries Eaten
Don	🍒 🍒 🍒 🍒 🍒
Eddie	🍒
Fred	🍒 🍒
🍒 = 3 cherries	

What's the Problem?

At the last basketball game, the players on the team scored the following points.

1. What is the range? ________
2. What is the mode? ________
3. How many players scored fewer than 10 points?

   ____

4. How many players scored more than 10 points?

   ____

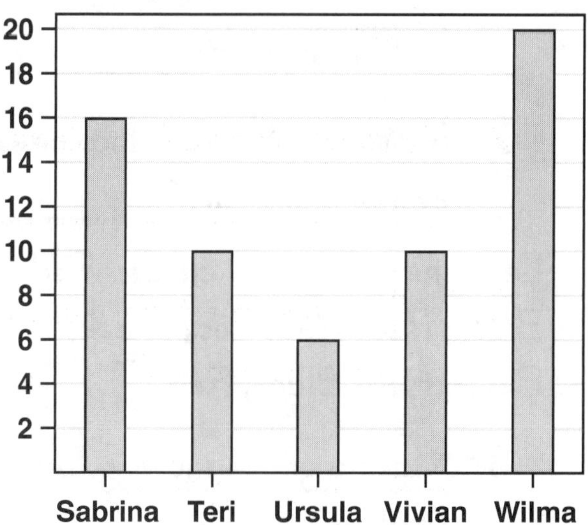

What's the Problem?

The museum collected the following admission tickets on opening day.

1. What is the difference between the number of adults and the number of children under 3 who came on opening day? ________
2. What is the range? ________
3. What is the mode? ________
4. How many teens came to the museum on opening day?

   ____

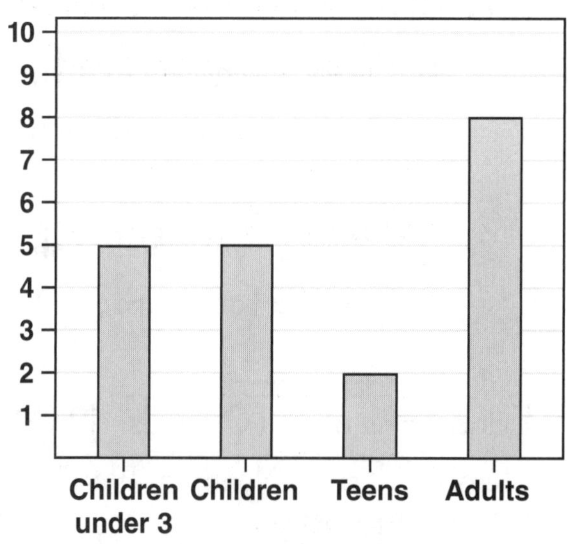

What's the Problem?

Leroy has a deck of 52 cards. Twenty-six cards are red and 26 cards are black.

1. Is it *likely* or *unlikely* that he will turn over a red card?_______________

2. Is it *likely* or *unlikely* that he will turn over a black card? _____________

Leroy turns over 10 cards: Red, Black, Red, Red, Red, Black, Black, Red, Black, Red.

3. Make a graph showing Leroy's findings.

What's the Problem?

Edna has a deck of 52 cards. Forty of the cards are numbered cards. Twelve are face cards.

1. Is it *likely* or *unlikely* that she will turn over a numbered card?

   ____

2. Is it *likely* or *unlikely* that she will turn over a face card?

   ____

Edna turns over 10 cards: Number, Number, Face, Number, Number, Number, Number, Face, Face, Number.

3. Make a graph showing Edna's findings.

What's the Problem?

Ask 10 classmates to pick their favorite breakfast drink from the following choices: milk, water, or orange juice.

Make a graph showing your findings.

What's the Problem?

Ask 10 classmates to choose their favorite number from 1–9.

Make a graph showing your findings.

What's the Problem?

Trenton asked 10 classmates to name their favorite color. Five students chose blue, 3 chose red, and 2 chose black.

Show Trenton's findings on a graph.

What's the Problem?

Minnie asked 10 students their ages. Three students were 7 years old, three students were 8 years old, and four students were 9 years old.

Show Minnie's findings on a graph.

What's the Problem?

Determine the probability (*likely, unlikely*) of an event happening.

1. It will snow today.

   ____

2. It will rain at recess.

   ____

3. We will get a new student in class today.

   ____

Write an event that will *likely* happen today.

____

____

____

____

Warm-Up
200

What's the Problem?

Determine the probability (*likely, unlikely*) of an event happening.

1. I will go swimming today.

   ____

2. I will read a book.

   ____

3. I will eat lunch.

   ____

Write an event that will *unlikely* happen today.

____

____

____

____

What's the Problem?

Billy has two 6-sided dice.

1. If he rolls both dice, what are the possible outcomes?

____

____

____

2. How many possible outcomes are there?

____

Warm-Up 202

What's the Problem?

Henrietta has two 9-sided dice.

1. If she rolls both dice, what are the possible outcomes?

____

____

____

2. How many possible outcomes are there?

____

What's the Problem?

Ramona made a list of 10 students' ages. They are 8, 8, 6, 7, 6, 5, 7, 8, 7, and 8 years old.

1. What is the range? __________

2. What is the mode? __________

What's the Problem?

Jerry asked 10 classmates how many teeth they had lost. His classmates had lost 3, 4, 1, 5, 6, 3, 2, 1, 5, and 3 teeth.

1. What is the range? __________

2. What is the mode? __________

What's the Problem?

Look at the pictograph.

1. How many zippers and buttons are there in all?

   ____

2. Are there more scissors or more buttons?

   ____

3. How many more zippers than scissors are there?

   ____

Craft Materials	Number Available
Zippers	
Buttons	
Scissors	

What's the Problem?

Look at the pictograph.

1. How many pencils does Audrey have?

   ____

2. Who has 10 pencils?

   ____

3. How many more pencils does Teddy have than Audrey?

   ____

Person	Number of Pencils
Audrey	
Teddy	
Phil	
= 5 pencils	

What's the Problem?

Bob and Sara played the same game twice. Their results are shown in the chart below.

1. What was each player's total number of points?
   Bob: ________ Sara: ________
2. Who won the first game?
   ____
3. Who won the second game?
   ____

Person	Game 1 Points	Game 2 Points	Total Points
Bob	3	11	
Sara	8	9	

What's the Problem?

Ms. Brown's and Mr. Green's classes had a contest to see which class could collect the most items for recycling.

1. Which class collected the most cans? ____________
2. How many more newspapers than bottles did Ms. Brown's class collect? ____________
3. How many more bottles than cans did Mr. Green's class collect? ____________

Class	Cans Collected	Bottles Collected	Newspapers Collected
Ms. Brown's	341	344	623
Mr. Green's	242	653	231

What's the Problem?

Lee has a 6-sided die. The die has the numbers 1, 2, 3, 4, 5, and 6 on it.

1. What are Lee's chances of rolling an odd number?

____

Even Number	
Odd Number	

2. What are Lee's chances of rolling an even number?

____

Roll a 6-sided die 10 times and record your results on the chart above.

3. Were your answers similar to #1 and #2? Why or why not?

____

What's the Problem?

Maxine has a 9-sided die. The die has the numbers 1, 2, 3, 4, 5, 6, 7, 8, and 9 on it.

1. What are Maxine's chances of rolling an odd number?

____

Even Number	
Odd Number	

2. What are Maxine's chances of rolling an even number?

____

Roll a 9-sided die 10 times and record your results on the chart above.

3. Were your answers similar to #1 and #2? Why or why not?

____

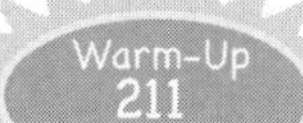

What's the Problem?

Work It Out

Mrs. McDonald wrote the following pattern on the board.

6, 13, 20, 27, ____, ____, ____

1. What are the next 3 numbers?
2. What is the rule?

____

WRITE ABOUT IT

____

____

What's the Problem?

Work It Out

Taryn wrote a pattern. The numbers increased by 5 each time.

What did Taryn's pattern look like?

____

WRITE ABOUT IT

____

____

What's the Problem?

Work It Out

If this pattern continues to 20 places, how many of each shape will be used?

____, ____, ____,

____, ____, ____, ____, ____

WRITE ABOUT IT

Warm-Up 214

What's the Problem?

Work It Out

Use 4 different shapes to make a pattern.

Use letters to describe the pattern you made.

WRITE ABOUT IT

What's the Problem?

Work It Out

Toby used blocks to build a pyramid. In the first row, he used 1 block. In the second row, he used 3 blocks. In the third row, he used 5 blocks.

1. How many blocks did Toby use in the seventh row? ________

2. How many blocks did Toby use in all 7 rows? ________

WRITE ABOUT IT

____

____

Warm-Up 216

What's the Problem?

Work It Out

Jenny put 1 seed in the first pot, 2 seeds in the second pot, and 3 seeds in the third pot.

1. If Jenny continues to put seeds in pots in this pattern, how many seeds will she put in the fifth pot? ________

2. How many seeds will Jenny put in all 5 pots? ________

WRITE ABOUT IT

____

____

What's the Problem?

Work It Out

Carol made the following pattern.

1, 2, 4, 8, 16, ____, ____, ____

1. What will the next 3 numbers be?
2. What is the rule?

____

WRITE ABOUT IT

____

____

Warm-Up 218

What's the Problem?

Work It Out

Michael wrote the following numbers.

500, 450, 400, 350, ____, ____, ____

1. What will the next 3 numbers be?
2. What is the rule?

____

WRITE ABOUT IT

____

____

Warm-Up 219

What's the Problem?

Work It Out

Show 8 ways to make the sum of 10, adding 3 different numbers (0–9).

Example: 0 + 1 + 9 = 10

WRITE ABOUT IT

Warm-Up 220

What's the Problem?

Work It Out

Show 10 ways to make the sum of 12, adding 3 different numbers (0–9).

Example: 0 + 3 + 9 = 12

WRITE ABOUT IT

Warm-Up 221

What's the Problem?

Work It Out

Write 3 addition facts with a sum of 8.

____

____

____

WRITE ABOUT IT

Warm-Up 222

What's the Problem?

Work It Out

Write 3 addition facts with a sum of 15.

____

____

____

WRITE ABOUT IT

Warm-Up 223

What's the Problem?

Write 3 subtraction facts with a difference of 5.

Work It Out

WRITE ABOUT IT

Warm-Up 224

What's the Problem?

Write 3 subtraction facts with a difference of 10.

Work It Out

WRITE ABOUT IT

What's the Problem?

Work It Out

Steven has 10 cars, 6 gliders, and 4 monster trucks.

What number sentence should Steven write to show how many cars and monster trucks he has in all?

____

WRITE ABOUT IT

____

____

Warm-Up 226

What's the Problem?

Work It Out

Wendy has 5 hair bows, 6 pairs of earrings, and 9 necklaces.

What number sentence should Wendy write to show how many earrings and necklaces she has in all?

____

WRITE ABOUT IT

____

____

What's the Problem?

Work It Out

Sam used a square, a circle, and a rectangle to make a repeating pattern.

What could Sam's pattern look like?

Use numbers to label the pattern.

WRITE ABOUT IT

Warm-Up 228

What's the Problem?

Work It Out

Molly used a triangle, a circle, and a pentagon to make a growing pattern.

What could Molly's pattern look like?

Use letters to label the pattern.

WRITE ABOUT IT

Warm-Up 229

What's the Problem?

Work It Out

Judy used the numbers 42 and 31 to make 2 addition problems.

What 2 addition problems could Judy make?

____

____

WRITE ABOUT IT

Warm-Up 230

What's the Problem?

Work It Out

Frank used the numbers 50 and 17 to make 2 addition problems.

What 2 addition problems could Frank make?

____

____

WRITE ABOUT IT

Warm-Up 231

What's the Problem?

Work It Out

Solve the following problems. Explain what strategy you used to solve the problems.

1. $3 + x = 9$
2. $4 + x = 12$
3. $x + 6 = 11$
4. $x + 6 = 15$

WRITE ABOUT IT

Warm-Up 232

What's the Problem?

Work It Out

Solve the following problems. Explain what strategy you used to solve the problems.

1. $4 + x = 15$
2. $x + 2 = 13$
3. $x + 7 = 14$
4. $9 + x = 9$

WRITE ABOUT IT

Warm-Up 233

What's the Problem?

Work It Out

Solve each problem. Write the inverse problem.

Example: Because 1 + 5 = 6, 6 – 5 = 1.

1. Because 3 + 7 = ______, ______________________.
2. Because 5 + 8 = ______, ______________________.
3. Because 9 + 3 = ______, ______________________.
4. Because 2 + 7 = ______, ______________________.

WRITE ABOUT IT

____

____

Warm-Up 234

What's the Problem?

Work It Out

Solve each problem. Write the inverse problem.

Example: Because 12 + 5 = 17, 17 – 5 = 12.

1. Because 11 + 4 = ______, ______________________.
2. Because 12 + 3 = ______, ______________________.
3. Because 8 + 10 = ______, ______________________.
4. Because 13 + 5 = ______, ______________________.

WRITE ABOUT IT

____

____

Warm-Up 235

What's the Problem?

Work It Out

April is trying to add the numbers 139, 27, and 1.

What is the easiest way for April to find the sum of the numbers?

____

____

WRITE ABOUT IT

Warm-Up 236

What's the Problem?

Work It Out

Brent counted 40 butterflies, 123 bees, and 7 ladybugs.

What is the easiest way for Brent to find the sum of the insects?

____

____

WRITE ABOUT IT

Warm-Up 237

What's the Problem?

Work It Out

Gus has the numbers 20, 6, and 4.

What are 2 ways Gus could group the numbers before adding them?

____

____

WRITE ABOUT IT

Warm-Up 238

What's the Problem?

Work It Out

Julie has the numbers 71, 4, and 10.

What are 2 ways Julie could group the numbers before adding them?

____

____

WRITE ABOUT IT

Warm-Up 239

What's the Problem?

Work It Out

Tyler is 12. Tyler's sister is older than he is. Together their ages equal 26.

Write the math equation that represents this problem.

____

WRITE ABOUT IT

____

____

Warm-Up 240

What's the Problem?

Work It Out

Georgina had 25 goldfish. She gave some to her friend. Now she has 11 goldfish.

Write the math equation that represents this problem.

____

WRITE ABOUT IT

____

____

Warm-Up 241

What's the Problem?

Work It Out

Thomas bought a pack of 3 pencils for 30 cents.

How much does 1 pencil cost?

____

WRITE ABOUT IT

____

____

Warm-Up 242

What's the Problem?

Work It Out

Pamela can buy 2 packs of gum for 40 cents or 3 packs of gum for 45 cents.

Which purchase is the better bargain?

____

WRITE ABOUT IT

____

____

Warm-Up 243

What's the Problem?

Work It Out

Tammy has this math problem:

$3 + a = 7$

$3 + a + b = 11$

What is the value of ***a***? ______

What is the value of ***b***? ______

WRITE ABOUT IT

Warm-Up 244

What's the Problem?

Work It Out

Brandon has this math problem:

$a + 5 = 9$

$b + 5 + a = 12$

What is the value of ***a***? ______

What is the value of ***b***? ______

WRITE ABOUT IT

Warm-Up 245

What's the Problem?

What is the missing addend in each equation?

Work It Out

1. 4 + 7 = ________ + 2 + 5
2. 3 + 2 + 5 = ________ + 5
3. 6 + 9 = ________ + 5 + 4
4. 1 + 11 = 0 + ________ + 1

WRITE ABOUT IT

____

____

Warm-Up 246

What's the Problem?

What is the missing addend in each equation?

Work It Out

1. 6 + 7 + 2 = ________ + 9
2. 13 + 1 + 0 = 1 + ________
3. 8 + 4 = ________ + 6
4. 9 + 3 + 3 = ________ + 6

WRITE ABOUT IT

____

____

Warm-Up 247

What's the Problem?

Work It Out

Wes had 12 watches. He sold some of them at the swap meet and bought 3 more. Now Wes has 9 watches.

How many watches did he sell at the swap meet? __________

Write the equation and solve the problem.

WRITE ABOUT IT

____

____

Warm-Up 248

What's the Problem?

Work It Out

Aubrey had 25 keys to put on her key ring. She dropped 10 keys on the ground. Then she found some of the keys. Aubrey now has 18 keys.

How many keys did she find? ________

Write the equation and solve the problem.

WRITE ABOUT IT

____

____

Warm-Up 249

What's the Problem?

Amanda wrote an equation. Unfortunately, she left out the operation signs (+ or –).

Insert the correct signs to make the equation true.

Work It Out

13 _____ 7 _____ 5 = 15

WRITE ABOUT IT

____

____

Warm-Up 250

What's the Problem?

Ivan wrote an equation, but he forgot to write the operation signs (+ or –).

Insert the correct signs to make the equation true.

Work It Out

9 _____ 9 _____ 9 = 27

WRITE ABOUT IT

____

____

ANSWER KEY

Warm-Up 1

Work It Out

1	2	3	4	5	6	7	8	9	10
11	12	13	14	15	16	17	18	19	20
21	22	23	24	25	26	27	28	29	30
31	32	33	34	35	36	37	38	39	40
41	42	43	44	45	46	47	48	49	50
51	52	53	54	55	56	57	58	59	60
61	62	63	64	65	66	67	68	69	70
71	72	73	74	75	76	77	78	79	80
81	82	83	(84)	85	86	87	88	89	90
91	92	93	94	95	96	97	98	99	100

8 + 4 = 12

Problem Solved

From the clues, we know that the number must start and end with 2, 4, 6, or 8 (the number has 2 even digits). The mystery number is 84 (the number in the tens place is greater than the number in the ones place; the sum of both digits is 12).

Warm-Up 2

Work It Out

April

SUNDAY	MONDAY	TUESDAY	WEDNESDAY	THURSDAY	FRIDAY	SATURDAY
					1	2
3	(4)	(5)	(6)	(7)	8	9
10	(11)	(12)	(13)	(14)	15	16
17	(18)	(19)	(20)	(21)	22	23
24	(25)	(26)	(27)	(28)	29	30

4 + 4 + 4 + 4 = 16

Problem Solved

Avonlea will have 16 nights of homework this month.

Warm-Up 3

Work It Out

☆ = 5 ☆ = 5 ☆ = 5 ☆ = 5

☆ = 5 ☆ = 5 ☆ = 5 ☆ = 5

5 + 5 + 5 + 5 + 5 + 5 + 5 + 5 = 40

Problem Solved

Eight stars will have 40 points.

Warm-Up 4

Work It Out

Tad	Phil	Tiffany	Amy	Fred
1st	**2nd**	**3rd**	**4th**	**5th**

Problem Solved

From the clues, we know that Tad is in the 1st seat (first). Fred is in the 5th seat (last). Phil is in the 2nd seat (behind Tad but before Tiffany). Tiffany is in the 3rd seat (between Phil and Amy). Amy is in the 4th seat.

Warm-Up 5

Work It Out

G G G G

G G G G

G + G + G + G + G + G + G + G = 8 Gs

Problem Solved

Drew will paint 8 green boards.

Warm-Up 6

Work It Out

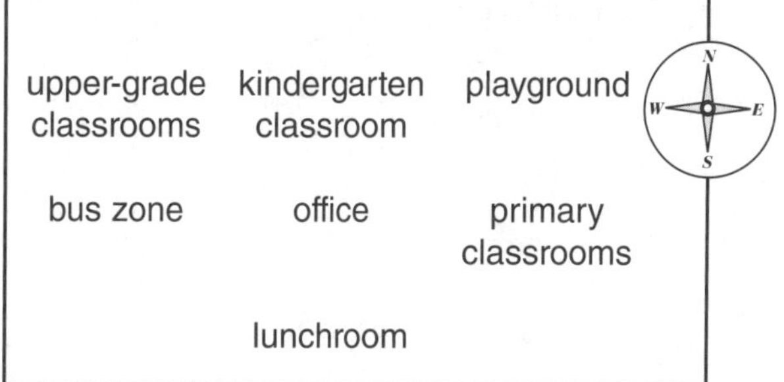

Problem Solved

Check to make sure the student has mapped the 7 locations correctly.

ANSWER KEY *(cont.)*

Warm-Up 7

Work It Out

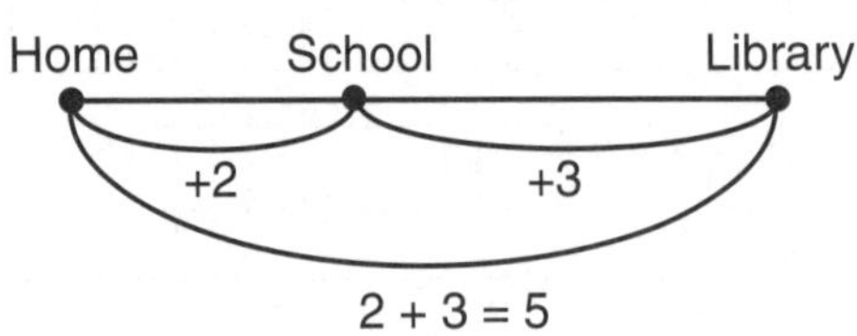

2 + 3 = 5

2 + 3 + 5 = 10

Problem Solved

Cindy walked 10 blocks in all.

Warm-Up 8

Work It Out

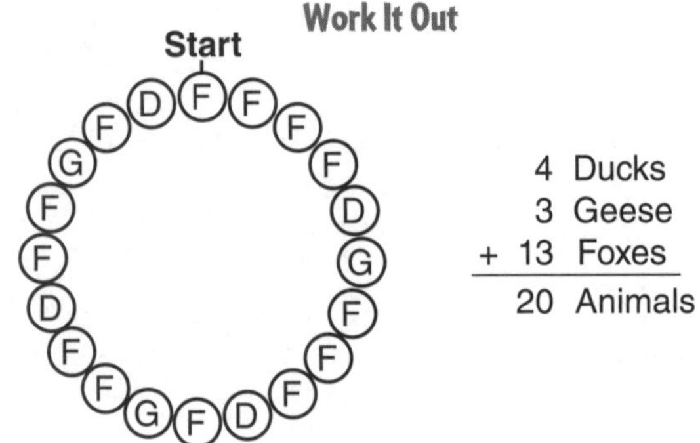

Problem Solved

From the clues, we know that 4 animals are ducks: #5, #10, #15, and #20 (every fifth animal is a duck). Three animals are geese: #6, #12, and #18 (every sixth animal is a goose). Thirteen animals are foxes (the remaining animals are foxes; 4 ducks + 3 geese + 13 foxes = 20 animals).

Warm-Up 9

Work It Out

1 + 2 + 3 + 4 + 5 + 6 = 21

Problem Solved

There are 21 dots on a 6-sided die.

Warm-Up 10

Work It Out

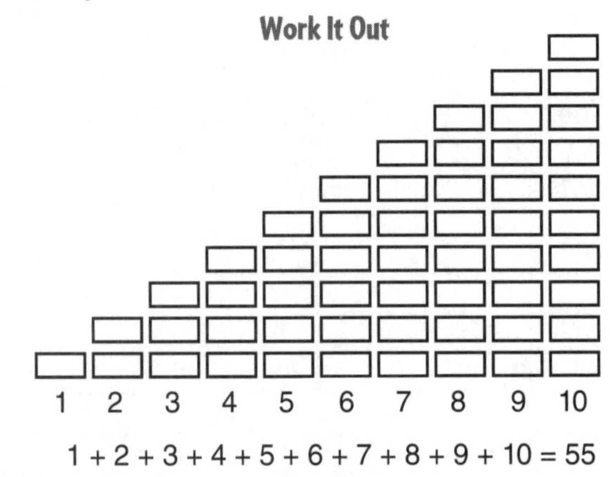

1 + 2 + 3 + 4 + 5 + 6 + 7 + 8 + 9 + 10 = 55

Problem Solved

Candy will use 55 bricks to make 10 columns.

Warm-Up 11

Work It Out

3 + 3 + 3 + 3 = 12

Problem Solved

Levi used 12 sunflowers.

Warm-Up 12

Work It Out

1. (H)(H)(H)
2. (T)(T)(T)
3. (H)(H)(T)
4. (H)(T)(H)
5. (T)(H)(H)
6. (H)(T)(T)
7. (T)(H)(T)
8. (T)(T)(H)

Problem Solved

The pennies could land 8 different ways (or as 4 unique combinations): 3 heads (HHH), 3 tails (TTT), 2 heads and 1 tails (HHT, HTH, or THH), and 1 heads and 2 tails (HTT, THT, or TTH).

ANSWER KEY *(cont.)*

Warm-Up 13

Work It Out

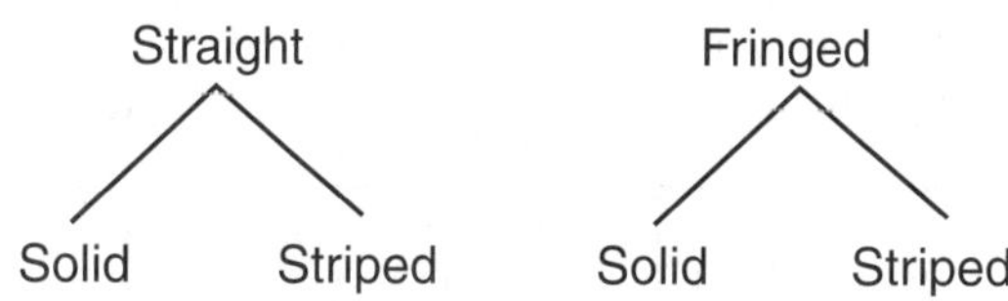

Problem Solved

Beth could make 4 scarves: straight ends with solid fleece, straight ends with striped fleece, fringed ends with solid fleece, fringed ends with striped fleece.

Warm-Up 14

Work It Out

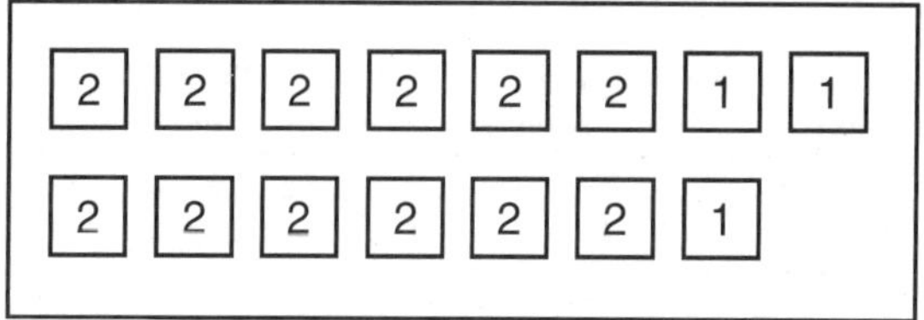

2 (students per seat) x 12 (seats) = 24 students

1 (adult per seat) x 3 (seats) = 3 adults

Problem Solved

All 15 seats will be used. Twelve seats will be used for the 24 students, and 3 seats will be used for the 3 adults.

Warm-Up 15

Work It Out

Sample answers:

Number of Pennies	Number of Nickels	Number of Dimes	Number of Quarters	Total Value
5	2	1	2	75 cents
10	6	1	1	75 cents
15	1	3	1	75 cents
20	4	1	1	75 cents
25	1	2	1	75 cents
30	2	1	1	75 cents
35	1	1	1	75 cents
25	3	1	1	75 cents

Problem Solved

Answers will vary. See above table for possible answers.

Warm-Up 16

Work It Out

Evan's Age	Rachel's Age
6 years old	15 years old
7 years old	16 years old
8 years old	17 years old
9 years old	18 years old

Problem Solved

When Evan is 9 years old (or half as old as his sister), Rachel will be 18 years old.

Warm-Up 17

Work It Out

Number of Girls	Number of Boys	Total Number of Students
4	8	12
5	10	15
6	12	18
7	14	21

Problem Solved

There are 14 boys and 7 girls in the class.

Warm-Up 18

Work It Out

Number of Salads	Number of Raisins	Number of Cherries	Number of Grapes	Total Pieces of Fruit
1	1	2	4	7
2	2	4	8	14
3	3	6	12	21

Problem Solved

Three fruit salads can be made.

ANSWER KEY *(cont.)*

Warm-Up 19

Work It Out

Week Number	Minutes Ran
1	10
2	14
3	18
4	22
5	26
6	30

Problem Solved

It will take 6 weeks before Dean is able to run for 30 minutes.

Warm-Up 20

Work It Out

Number of Tricycles	1	2	3	4	5	6	7	8
Number of Wheels	3	6	9	12	15	18	21	24

Problem Solved

There are 24 wheels on 8 tricycles.

Warm-Up 21

Work It Out

1st Scoop	2nd Scoop	3rd Scoop
V	C	S
V	S	C
C	S	V
C	V	S
S	V	C
S	C	V

Problem Solved

The scoops can be stacked 6 different ways: vanilla, chocolate, strawberry; vanilla, strawberry, chocolate; chocolate, strawberry, vanilla; chocolate, vanilla, strawberry; strawberry, vanilla, chocolate; strawberry, chocolate, vanilla.

Warm-Up 22

Work It Out

Number of Hamsters	Number of Parrots	Number of Rabbits	Total Number of Animals
1	3	6	10
2	4	7	13
3	5	8	16
4	6	9	19
5	7	10	22
6	8	11	25

$6 + 8 + 11 = 25$

Problem Solved

The Pet Store has 6 hamsters, 8 parrots, and 11 rabbits.

Warm-Up 23

Work It Out

In	Out
3	**7**
8	12
9	13
6	10
1	5
0	**4**
5	**9**
2	6
4	8

Problem Solved

The rule is to add 4 to each "In" number or to subtract 4 from each "Out" number.

Warm-Up 24

Work It Out

Person or Group Number	1	2	3	4	5
Number of People	1	4	7	10	13

Problem Solved

The fifth group will have 13 people.

ANSWER KEY *(cont.)*

Warm-Up 25

Work It Out

Day Number	1	2	3	4	5
Number of Bones	1	8	15	22	29

1 + 8 + 15 + 22 + 29 = 75

Problem Solved

Barney ate 1 bone on Day 1, 8 bones on Day 2, 15 bones on Day 3, 22 bones on Day 4, and 29 bones on Day 5.

Warm-Up 26

Work It Out

Number of Swing Sets	Number of Swings
1	3
2	6
3	9
4	12
5	15
6	18

Problem Solved

The principal should order 6 swing sets.

Warm-Up 27

Work It Out

Students can use manipulatives, such as the ones shown on page 39, to determine if 50 counters will fit in their pencil boxes.

Problem Solved

Answers will vary.

Warm-Up 28

Work It Out

Sample answers:

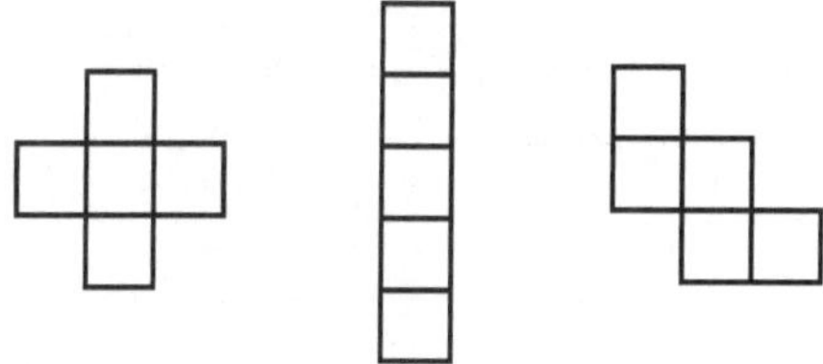

Problem Solved

Check to make sure the student drew 5 squares that touch on at least one side.

Warm-Up 29

Work It Out

Students can use pencils to act out this math problem.

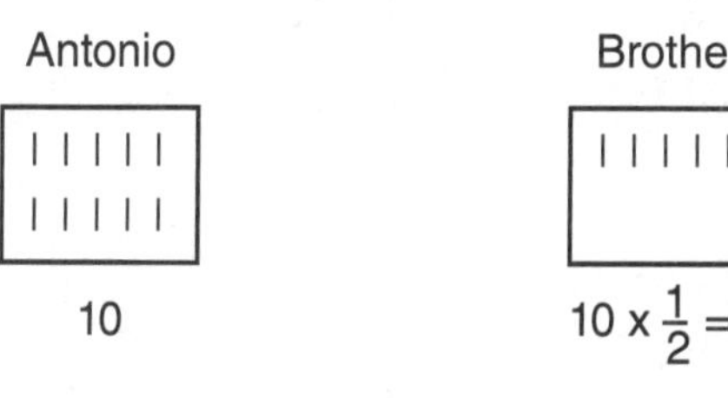

$10 \times \frac{1}{2} = 5$

10 + 5 = 15

Problem Solved

Antonio has 10 pencils and his brother has 5 pencils. They have 15 pencils in all.

Warm-Up 30

Work It Out

Students can look at an analog clock to determine the correct answer.

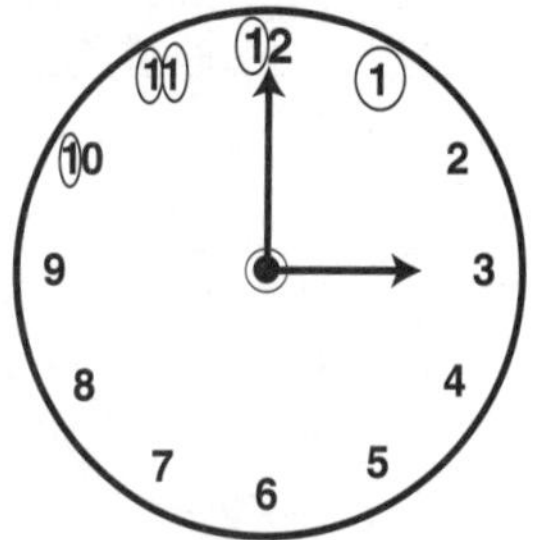

Problem Solved

There are five 1s on the face of a clock.

ANSWER KEY *(cont.)*

Warm-Up 31

Work It Out

Students can fold a piece of paper to determine how many squares there are.

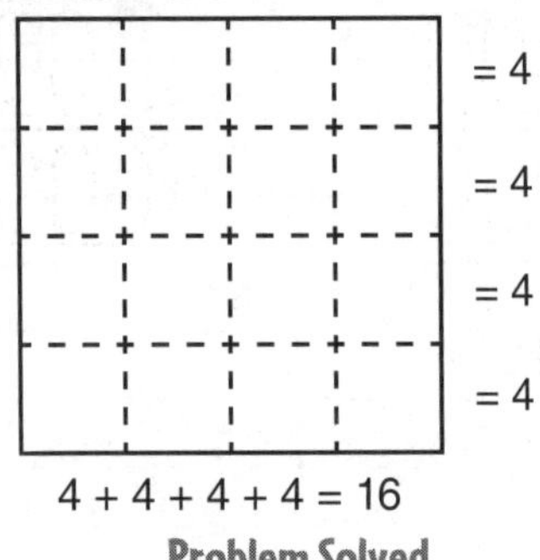

4 + 4 + 4 + 4 = 16

Problem Solved

Marcy will have 16 squares.

Warm-Up 32

Work It Out

Students can measure and cut string to determine the correct answer.

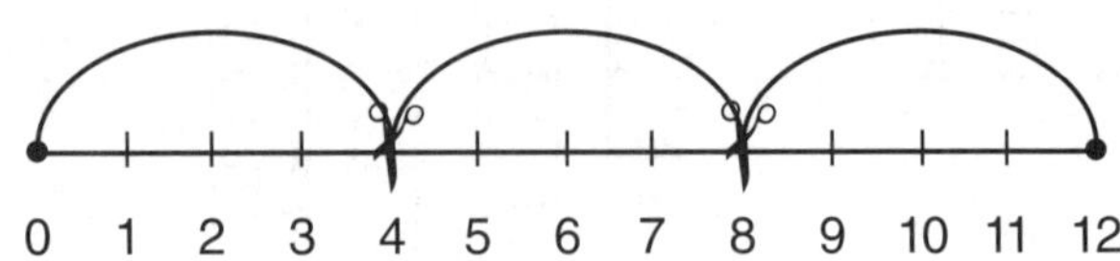

Problem Solved

Each piece of string is 4 inches long. Jeremiah made 2 cuts.

Warm-Up 33

Work It Out

Students can use circle-shaped cutouts or manipulatives to act out this math problem.

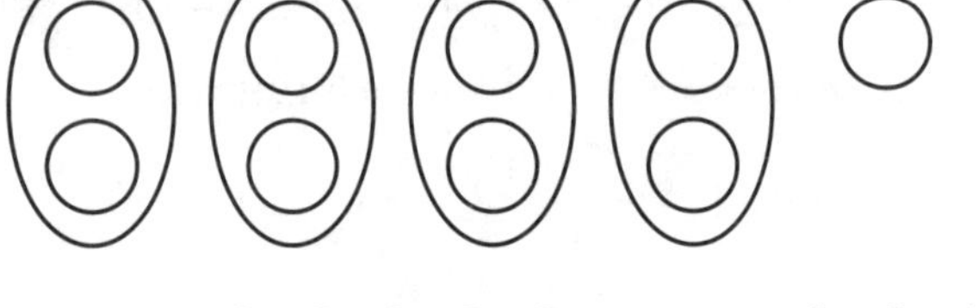

2 + 2 + 2 + 2 = 8 9 – 8 = 1

Problem Solved

Each person will get 2 cookies. There will be 1 cookie left over.

Warm-Up 34

Work It Out

Students can use manipulatives to act out this problem.

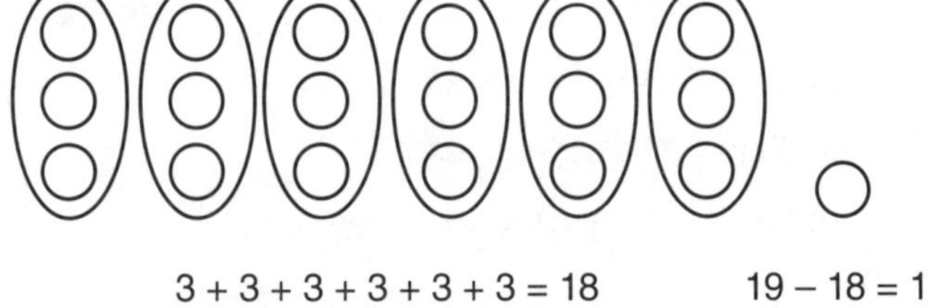

3 + 3 + 3 + 3 + 3 + 3 = 18 19 – 18 = 1

Problem Solved

No, Sela will not end up with 0 counters. She will have 1 counter left over.

Warm-Up 35

Work It Out

Students can use circle-shaped cutouts and scissors to act out this problem.

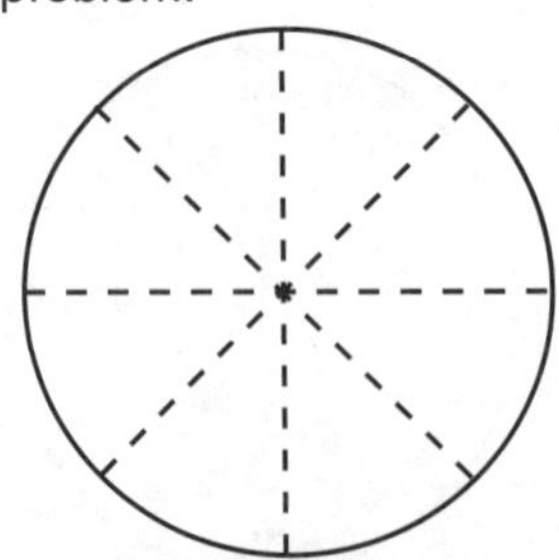

Problem Solved

Mark will make 4 straight cuts.

Warm-Up 36

Work It Out

Students can write numbers or use a set of number cards (1–20) to act out this problem.

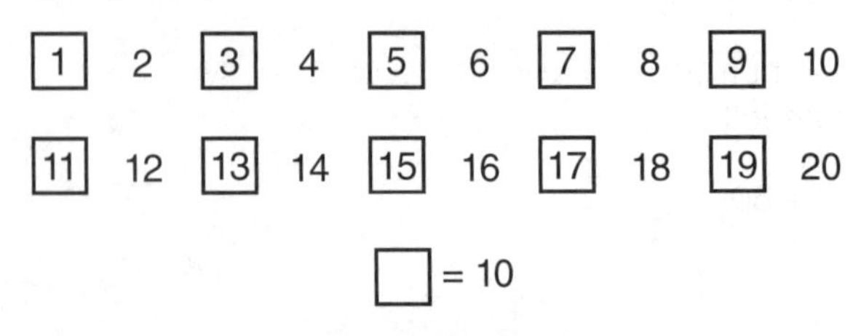

Problem Solved

Bettina wrote 10 odd numbers: 1, 3, 5, 7, 9, 11, 13, 15, 17, 19.

ANSWER KEY *(cont.)*

Warm-Up 37

Work It Out

Students can use rectangle-shaped cutouts (to represent playing cards) to act out this problem.

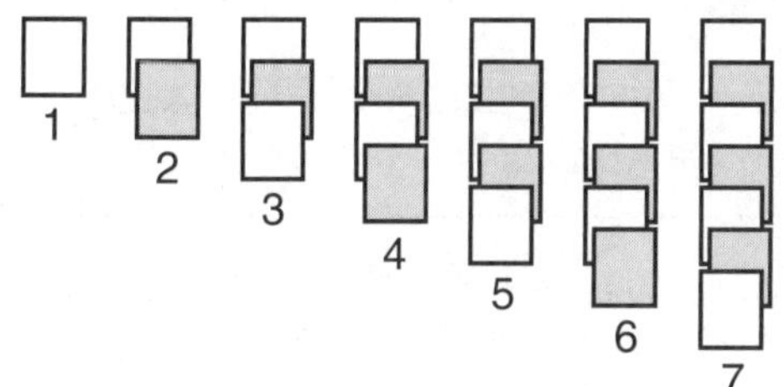

1 + 2 + 3 + 4 + 5 + 6 + 7 = 28

Problem Solved

There will be 7 cards in the last stack. Molly will use 28 cards in all.

Warm-Up 38

Work It Out

Students can use small manipulatives to act out this problem.

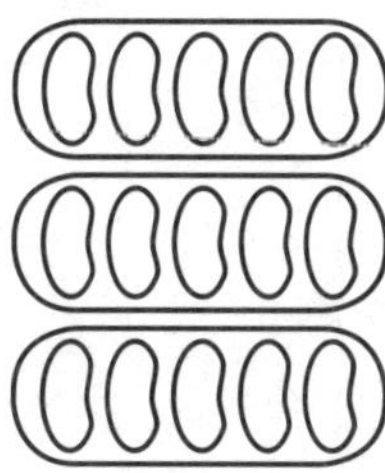

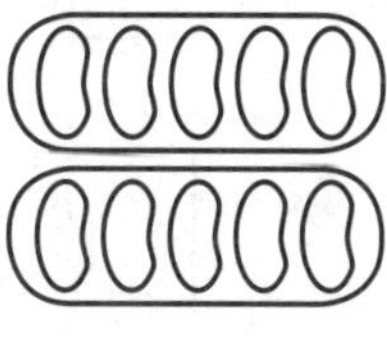

5 + 5 + 5 + 5 + 5 = 25

Problem Solved

Wally put 5 jelly beans in each group.

Warm-Up 39

Work It Out

Students can make an educated guess, check it for accuracy, and continue making guesses until reaching the correct answer.

3 zebras + 3 more flamingos = 6 flamingos

6 flamingos x 2 flamingo legs = 12 flamingo legs

3 zebras x 4 zebra legs = 12 zebra legs

Problem Solved

Zoe counted 6 flamingos and 3 zebras.

Warm-Up 40

Work It Out

Students can make an educated guess, check it for accuracy, and continue making guesses until reaching the correct answer.

36 black keys + 16 more white keys = 52 white keys

36 black keys + 52 white keys = 88 total keys

Problem Solved

A piano has 52 white keys. A piano has 36 black keys.

Warm-Up 41

Work It Out

Students can make an educated guess, check it for accuracy, and continue making guesses until reaching the correct answer.

The numbers 49 and 50 are consecutive (one follows the other).

49 + 50 = 99

Problem Solved

Lexi found that the numbers 49 and 50 have the sum of 99.

Warm-Up 42

Work It Out

Students can make an educated guess, check it for accuracy, and continue making guesses until reaching the correct answer.

Sample answer:

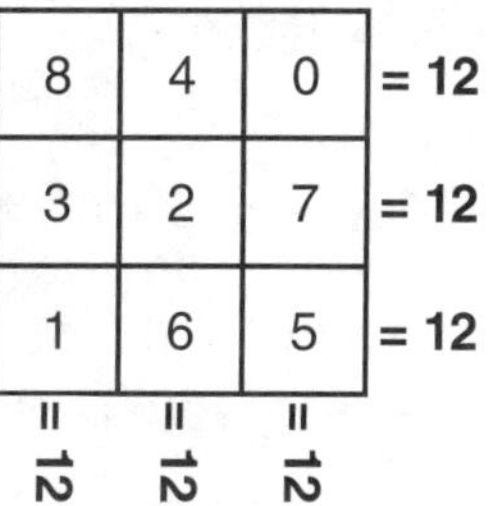

8	4	0	= 12
3	2	7	= 12
1	6	5	= 12
= 12	= 12	= 12	

Problem Solved

Check to make sure that each row and column has a sum of 12.

ANSWER KEY *(cont.)*

Warm-Up 43

Work It Out

Students can make an educated guess, check it for accuracy, and continue making guesses until reaching the correct answer.

30 pounds x 2 = 60 pounds

60 pounds + 30 pounds = 90 pounds

Problem Solved

The dog weighs 60 pounds, and the cat weighs 30 pounds.

Warm-Up 44

Work It Out

Students can make an educated guess, check it for accuracy, and continue making guesses until reaching the correct answer.

6 starfish + 2 more octopuses = 8 octopuses

6 starfish + 8 octopuses = 14 animals

Problem Solved

There were 8 octopuses. There were 6 starfish.

Warm-Up 45

Work It Out

Students can make an educated guess, check it for accuracy, and continue making guesses until reaching the correct answer.

2 x 4-pack light bulbs = 8 light bulbs

5 x 5-pack light bulbs = 25 light bulbs

8 light bulbs + 25 light bulbs = 33 light bulbs

2 packs + 5 packs = 7 packs

Problem Solved

Melanie needs to buy two 4-packs of light bulbs and five 5-packs of light bulbs. She needs to buy 7 packs in all.

Warm-Up 46

Work It Out

Students can make an educated guess, check it for accuracy, and continue making guesses until reaching the correct answer.

2 x 1 penny (1 cent each) = 2 cents

1 x 1 nickel (5 cents each) = 5 cents

2 x 2 quarters (25 cents each) = 50 cents

2 + 1 + 2 = 5 coins

Problem Solved

Sarah has 2 pennies, 1 nickel, and 2 quarters.

Warm-Up 47

Work It Out

Students can make an educated guess, check it for accuracy, and continue making guesses until reaching the correct answer.

5 squash + 10 more cucumbers = 15 cucumbers

15 cucumbers + 5 squash = 20 vegetables

Problem Solved

Heath picked 15 cucumbers and 5 squash.

Warm-Up 48

Work It Out

Students can make an educated guess, check it for accuracy, and continue making guesses until reaching the correct answer.

The numbers 31, 33, and 35 are in order when skip counting by 2s.

31 + 33 + 35 = 99

Problem Solved

Ian added 31, 33, and 35 together to make a sum of 99.

Warm-Up 49

Work It Out

Students can make an educated guess, check it for accuracy, and continue making guesses until reaching the correct answer.

3 pentagons x 5 pentagon sides = 15 pentagon sides

5 triangles x 3 triangle sides = 15 triangle sides

Problem Solved

Karen drew 3 pentagons and 5 triangles.

Warm-Up 50

Work It Out

Students can make an educated guess, check it for accuracy, and continue making guesses until reaching the correct answer.

Sample answer:

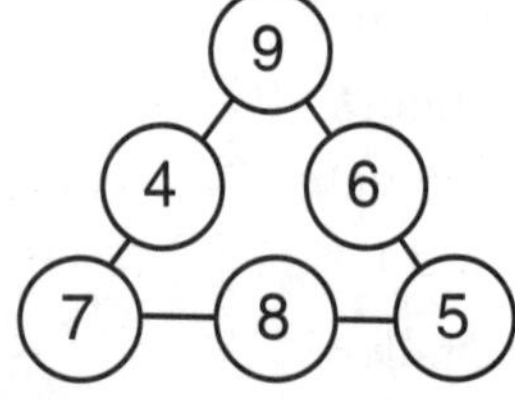

Problem Solved

Check to make sure each side of the triangle has the sum of 20.

ANSWER KEY *(cont.)*

Warm-Up 51

Six different numbers can be made: 12, 18, 21, 28, 81, and 82.

Warm-Up 52

Six different numbers can be made: 128, 182, 218, 281, 812, and 821.

Warm-Up 53

Jenny is 3 years old, Seth is 6 years old, and Roger is 11 years old.

Warm-Up 54

8 people

Warm-Up 55

70 tulips

Warm-Up 56

32 juice boxes

Warm-Up 57

8 pencils

Warm-Up 58

4 newspapers

Warm-Up 59

Sample answers:

number word (*fifty-eight*)

numbers and words (5 *tens* 8 *ones*)

numbers (50 + 8)

place value blocks (5 ten rods and 8 ones)

Warm-Up 60

Sample answers:

number word (*one hundred thirty-nine*)

numbers and words (1 *hundred* 3 *tens* 9 *ones*)

numbers (100 + 30 + 9)

place value blocks (1 hundred flat, 3 ten rods, and 9 ones)

Warm-Up 61

Hunter

Warm-Up 62

6 chocolate, 4 vanilla, 2 strawberry

Warm-Up 63

125 pieces

Warm-Up 64

271 gumballs

Warm-Up 65

No, Sam is not correct. He made 52, not 62. He needs 1 more ten rod.

Warm-Up 66

Check to make sure the student has drawn 2 hundred flats and 7 ones.

Warm-Up 67

Check to make sure the student has written four of the following: 46, 48, 64, 68, 84, 86. (The numbers should be ordered from least to greatest.)

Warm-Up 68

Check to make sure the student has written four of the following: 135, 137, 153, 157, 173, 175, 315, 317, 351, 357, 371, 375, 513, 517, 531, 537, 571, 573, 713, 715, 731, 735, 751, 753. (The numbers should be ordered from greatest to least.)

Warm-Up 69

8 + 9 = 17	17 – 9 = 8
9 + 8 = 17	17 – 8 = 9

Warm-Up 70

6 + 14 = 20	20 – 6 = 14
14 + 6 = 20	20 – 14 = 6

Warm-Up 71

286 more blue candles

Warm-Up 72

258 more plums

Warm-Up 73

40 pieces of candy

Warm-Up 74

18 hats

Warm-Up 75

9 bows

Warm-Up 76

4 olives

Warm-Up 77

Six multiplication problems can be made:

1 x 2 = 2	5 x 1 = 5
2 x 1 = 2	2 x 5 = 10
1 x 5 = 5	5 x 2 = 10

Warm-Up 78

Twelve multiplication problems can be made:

1 x 2 = 2	1 x 10 = 10
2 x 1 = 2	10 x 1 = 10
1 x 5 = 5	2 x 10 = 20
5 x 1 = 5	10 x 2 = 20
2 x 5 = 10	5 x 10 = 50
5 x 2 = 10	10 x 5 = 50

Warm-Up 79

6 bracelets

Warm-Up 80

8 marbles

Warm-Up 81

6 slices

Warm-Up 82

15 pieces

Warm-Up 83

53 cents

Warm-Up 84

31 cents

Warm-Up 85

52 pencils

Warm-Up 86

33 stamps

Warm-Up 87

98 cents

Warm-Up 88

94 cents

ANSWER KEY *(cont.)*

Warm-Up 89

Three quarters is worth more than 6 dimes; 75 cents is greater than 60 cents.

Warm-Up 90

Two half-dollars is the same as 100 pennies; 100 cents is equal to 100 cents.

Warm-Up 91

4 sides, 4 corners

Warm-Up 92

6 sides, 6 corners

Warm-Up 93

2 triangles (diagonal line from top left to bottom right)
2 triangles (diagonal line from top right to bottom left)
2 vertical rectangles
2 horizontal rectangles

Warm-Up 94

3 vertical rectangles
3 horizontal rectangles

Warm-Up 95

Answers will vary.

Warm-Up 96

Answers will vary.

Warm-Up 97

rectangle

Warm-Up 98

4-sided shape = rectangle, trapezoid, or parallelogram
3-sided shape = triangle

Warm-Up 99

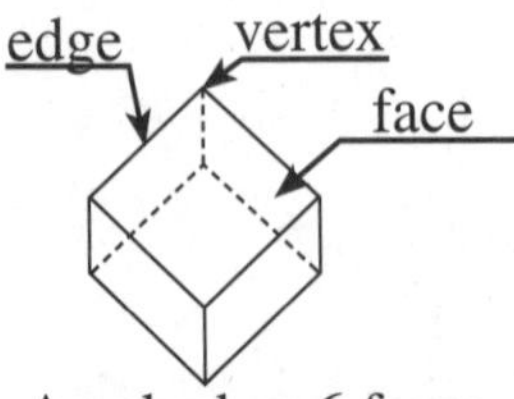

A cube has 6 faces.

Warm-Up 100

The edge is where 2 sides of a shape come together; the vertex is where sides come together to form a point.
A cube has 8 vertexes.
A cube has 12 edges.

Warm-Up 101

1. Carousel
2. Roller Coaster
3. Picnic Area

Warm-Up 102

Maps/answers will vary.

Warm-Up 103

1. J10	3. E2	5. C9	7. I1
2. F8	4. G5	6. A3	8. B6

Warm-Up 104

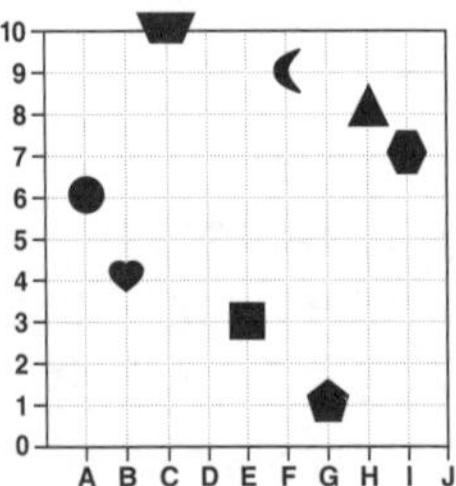

Warm-Up 105

1. behind
2. under
3. on top of (on)
4. beside (next to)

Warm-Up 106

Check to make sure the picture was drawn correctly.

Warm-Up 107

Sample answers:
Alike: A cube has faces that are in the shape of a square.
Different: A square is a plane shape (flat), while a cube is a geometric solid.

Warm-Up 108

Sample answers:
Alike: A triangular pyramid has faces that are in the shape of a triangle.
Different: A triangle is a plane shape (flat), while a triangular pyramid is a geometric solid.

Warm-Up 109

He will paint 24 cube faces red.
He will paint 36 cube faces yellow.

Warm-Up 110

He can write 20 names on the pyramids.

Warm-Up 111

a pentagon and a hexagon

Warm-Up 112

an octagon and an oval

Warm-Up 113

Sliding Flipping Turning

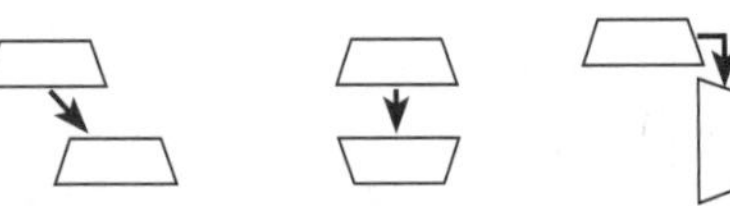

Warm-Up 114

Sliding Flipping Turning

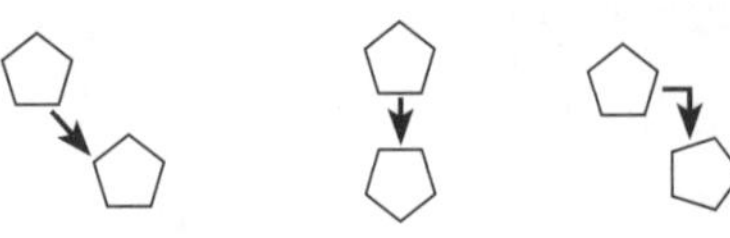

Warm-Up 115

Sample answers:
tissue box, toy box, blocks

Warm-Up 116

Sample answers:
light fixture, ball, globe

Warm-Up 117

Check to make sure the student's triangle is the same size as the one already on the paper.

Warm-Up 118

Check to make sure the student's trapezoid is the same size as the one already on the paper.

Warm-Up 119

Sample answers:
Sort by round faces, number of faces, or number of corners.

ANSWER KEY *(cont.)*

Warm-Up 120

Sample answers:

Stacking shapes: cube, cylinder, rectangular prism

Rolling shapes: sphere, cone, cylinder

Stacking and rolling shape: cylinder

Warm-Up 121

Charles; octagon

Warm-Up 122

a circle

Warm-Up 123

Check to make sure the student drew a shape or design and wrote the correct coordinate points.

Warm-Up 124

Check to make sure the student drew a letter and wrote the correct coordinate points.

Warm-Up 125

The perimeter is 16. The area is also 16.

Warm-Up 126

The perimeter is 16. The area is 12.

Warm-Up 127

Check to make sure the student drew the reflection of his or her phone number correctly.

Sample answer:

867-5309 → 9035-768

Warm-Up 128

Check to make sure the student drew the flip of his or her name correctly.

Sample answer:

Kim → miK

Warm-Up 129

Warm-Up 130

Warm-Up 131

3 inches

Warm-Up 132

12 lines

Warm-Up 133

30 minutes

Warm-Up 134

8:20 a.m.

Warm-Up 135

11:00 p.m.

Warm-Up 136

8:35 a.m.

Warm-Up 137

12 inches

Warm-Up 138

36 inches

Warm-Up 139

66 days

Warm-Up 140

Thursday, November 25

Warm-Up 141

86°F

Warm-Up 142

41°F

Warm-Up 143

Bandit is 12 inches or 1 foot tall. Ranger is 16 inches or 1 foot, 4 inches tall.

Warm-Up 144

Homer's tail is 2 inches long.

Homer's body plus tail is $3\frac{1}{2}$ inches long.

Warm-Up 145

$1\frac{1}{2}$ inches

Warm-Up 146

The first piece of ribbon is 1 inch long. The second piece of ribbon is 2 inches long. The third piece of ribbon is 6 inches long.

Warm-Up 147

18 inches

Warm-Up 148

24 inches

Warm-Up 149

20 centimeters

Warm-Up 150

3-inch line

Warm-Up 151

Tina should use a cup because it measures the capacity of liquids.

Warm-Up 152

David should use a scale because it measures the weight of objects.

Warm-Up 153

Glenda should use a measuring tape (ruler, yardstick) to measure the height of the tree. The measuring tape can measure many feet at one time.

Warm-Up 154

Ricardo should measure the ant using a centimeter ruler. Ants are small, and centimeters can measure items that are small.

Warm-Up 155

52 squares

Warm-Up 156

Answers will vary. Check to make sure that the student colored in 30 squares.

ANSWER KEY *(cont.)*

Warm-Up 157
Answers will vary.

Warm-Up 158
Answers will vary.

Warm-Up 159
about 6 inches

Warm-Up 160
Answers will vary.

Warm-Up 161
Nine inches is less than 1 foot. One foot is 12 inches long.

Warm-Up 162
Answers will vary.

Warm-Up 163
5 minutes

Warm-Up 164
120 seconds

Warm-Up 165
15 minutes

Warm-Up 166
3 hours

Warm-Up 167
7:00 a.m.

Warm-Up 168
4:30 p.m.

Warm-Up 169
17 days

Warm-Up 170
about 12 weeks

Warm-Up 171

Favorite Book	Number of People
Mystery	II
History	III
Animals	~~IIII~~

Warm-Up 172

Type of Bag	Number of People
Carrying Backpack	~~IIII~~ I
Tote Bag	~~IIII~~ II
Rolling Backpack	~~IIII~~ III

Warm-Up 173

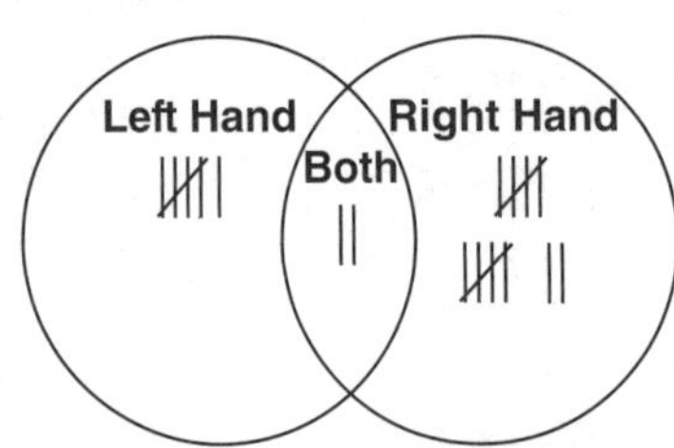

Warm-Up 174

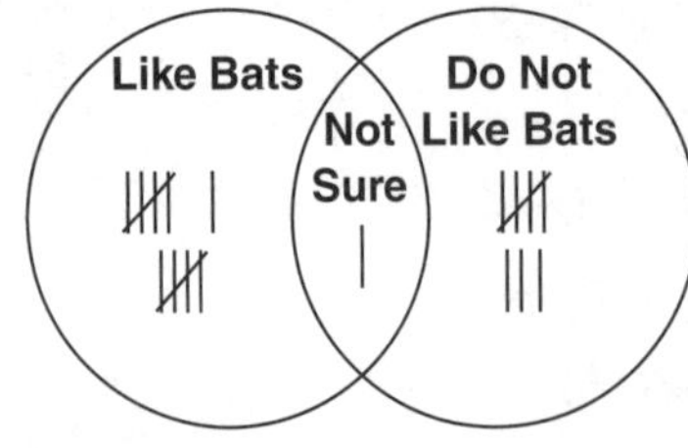

Warm-Up 175
Check to make sure the student made the correct bar graph.

Warm-Up 176
Check to make sure the student made the correct bar graph.

Warm-Up 177
Check to make sure the student made the correct bar graph.

Warm-Up 178
Check to make sure the student made the correct bar graph.

Warm-Up 179
Sample questions:

1. How many more students have only sisters than only brothers?
2. How many students are "only children"?

Warm-Up 180
Sample questions:

1. How many people said breakfast was their favorite meal?
2. Did more people pick lunch or dinner as their favorite meal?

Warm-Up 181
1. 5 2. 5

Warm-Up 182
1. 7 2. 6

Warm-Up 183
1. likely 2. unlikely

Warm-Up 184
1. likely 2. unlikely

Warm-Up 185

1. likely because 75% of the spinner is red
2. unlikely because only 25% of the spinner is blue

Warm-Up 186

1. likely because it's a fair spinner
2. likely because it's a fair spinner

Warm-Up 187
Check to make sure the student divided the spinner into four equal parts.
Sample answer: Yes, it is a fair spinner. Each space on the spinner is the same size. A player has an equal chance of landing on each of the 4 colors.

Warm-Up 188
Check to make sure the student colored the spinner so that it is mostly green.
Sample answer: No, it is not a fair spinner. Most of the spinner is green, and there are just small areas of the other 3 colors (less chance of landing on them).

ANSWER KEY *(cont.)*

Warm-Up 189

1. Callie
2. Brandy
3. 18 pie slices

Warm-Up 190

1. 9 cherries
2. Eddie
3. 24 cherries

Warm-Up 191

1. 14
2. 10
3. 1 player
4. 2 players

Warm-Up 192

1. 3 adults
2. 6
3. 5
4. 2 teens

Warm-Up 193

1. likely
2. likely
3. Check to make sure the student made a graph to show the results.

Warm-Up 194

1. likely
2. unlikely
3. Check to make sure the student made a graph to show the results.

Warm-Up 195

Check to make sure the student made a graph to show the results.

Warm-Up 196

Check to make sure the student made a graph to show the results.

Warm-Up 197

Check to make sure the student made a graph to show the results.

Warm-Up 198

Check to make sure the student made a graph to show the results.

Warm-Up 199

Answers will vary.

Warm-Up 200

Answers will vary.

Warm-Up 201

1. 1-1, 1-2, 1-3, 1-4, 1-5, 1-6, 2-1, 2-2, 2-3, 2-4, 2-5, 2-6, 3-1, 3-2, 3-3, 3-4, 3-5, 3-6, 4-1, 4-2, 4-3, 4-4, 4-5, 4-6, 5-1, 5-2, 5-3, 5-4, 5-5, 5-6, 6-1, 6-2, 6-3, 6-4, 6-5, 6-6
2. 36 possible outcomes

Warm-Up 202

1. 1-1, 1-2, 1-3, 1-4, 1-5, 1-6, 1-7, 1-8, 1-9, 2-1, 2-2, 2-3, 2-4, 2-5, 2-6, 2-7, 2-8, 2-9, 3-1, 3-2, 3-3, 3-4, 3-5, 3-6, 3-7, 3-8, 3-9, 4-1, 4-2, 4-3, 4-4, 4-5, 4-6, 4-7, 4-8, 4-9, 5-1, 5-2, 5-3, 5-4, 5-5, 5-6, 5-7, 5-8, 5-9, 6-1, 6-2, 6-3, 6-4, 6-5, 6-6, 6-7, 6-8, 6-9, 7-1, 7-2, 7-3, 7-4, 7-5, 7-6, 7-7, 7-8, 7-9, 8-1, 8-2, 8-3, 8-4, 8-5, 8-6, 8-7, 8-8, 8-9, 9-1, 9-2, 9-3, 9-4, 9-5, 9-6, 9-7, 9-8, 9-9
2. 81 possible outcomes

Warm-Up 203

1. 3
2. 8

Warm-Up 204

1. 5
2. 3

Warm-Up 205

1. 18 zippers and buttons
2. more buttons
3. 2 more zippers

Warm-Up 206

1. 15 pencils
2. Phil
3. 15 more pencils

Warm-Up 207

1. Bob—14 points; Sara—17 points
2. Sara
3. Bob

Warm-Up 208

1. Ms. Brown's
2. 279 more newspapers
3. 411 more bottles

Warm-Up 209

1. 3 out of 6, or $\frac{1}{2}$
2. 3 out of 6, or $\frac{1}{2}$
3. Check to make sure the student recorded his or her results in the chart. Answers will vary.

Warm-Up 210

1. 5 out of 9, or $\frac{5}{9}$
2. 4 out of 9, or $\frac{4}{9}$
3. Check to make sure the student recorded his or her results in the chart. Answers will vary.

Warm-Up 211

1. 34, 41, 48
2. add 7

Warm-Up 212

Patterns will vary, but the rule must be +5.

Warm-Up 213

7 circles, 3 hearts, 4 squares, 6 stars

Warm-Up 214

Patterns will vary.

Warm-Up 215

1. 13 blocks
2. 49 blocks

Warm-Up 216

1. 5 seeds
2. 15 seeds

Warm-Up 217

1. 32, 64, 128
2. double each number, or multiply by 2

Warm-Up 218

1. 300, 250, 200
2. subtract 50

ANSWER KEY *(cont.)*

Warm-Up 219

Sample answers:

$0 + 1 + 9 = 10$
$0 + 2 + 8 = 10$
$0 + 3 + 7 = 10$
$0 + 4 + 6 = 10$
$1 + 2 + 7 = 10$
$1 + 3 + 6 = 10$
$1 + 4 + 5 = 10$
$2 + 5 + 3 = 10$

Warm-Up 220

Sample answers:

$0 + 3 + 9 = 12$
$0 + 4 + 8 = 12$
$0 + 5 + 7 = 12$
$1 + 2 + 9 = 12$
$1 + 3 + 8 = 12$
$1 + 4 + 7 = 12$
$1 + 5 + 6 = 12$
$2 + 3 + 7 = 12$
$2 + 4 + 6 = 12$
$3 + 4 + 5 = 12$

Warm-Up 221

Sample answers:

$1 + 7 = 8$
$2 + 6 = 8$
$3 + 5 = 8$

Warm-Up 222

Sample answers:

$5 + 10 = 15$
$6 + 9 = 15$
$7 + 8 = 15$

Warm-Up 223

Sample answers:

$6 - 1 = 5$ $\quad$ $8 - 3 = 5$
$7 - 2 = 5$

Warm-Up 224

Sample answers:

$15 - 5 = 10$ $\quad$ $25 - 15 = 10$
$20 - 10 = 10$

Warm-Up 225

$10 + 4 = 14$ or $4 + 10 = 14$

Warm-Up 226

$6 + 9 = 15$ or $9 + 6 = 15$

Warm-Up 227

Patterns and labeling will vary. Check to make sure the student used numbers to label the repeating pattern.

Warm-Up 228

Patterns and labeling will vary. Check to make sure the student used letters to label the growing pattern.

Warm-Up 229

$42 + 31 = 73$
$31 + 42 = 73$

Warm-Up 230

$50 + 17 = 67$
$17 + 50 = 67$

Warm-Up 231

1. 6 2. 8 3. 5 4. 9

Check to make sure the student explained the strategy he or she used to solve the problems.

Warm-Up 232

1. 11 2. 11 3. 7 4. 0

Check to make sure the student explained the strategy he or she used to solve the problems.

Warm-Up 233

1. 10, then $10 - 7 = 3$ (or $10 - 3 = 7$)
2. 13, then $13 - 8 = 5$ (or $13 - 5 = 8$)
3. 12, then $12 - 3 = 9$ (or $12 - 9 = 3$)
4. 9, then $9 - 7 = 2$ (or $9 - 2 = 7$)

Warm-Up 234

1. 15, then $15 - 4 = 11$ (or $15 - 11 = 4$)
2. 15, then $15 - 3 = 12$ (or $15 - 12 = 3$)
3. 18, then $18 - 10 = 8$ (or $18 - 8 = 10$)
4. 18, then $18 - 5 = 13$ (or $18 - 13 = 5$)

Warm-Up 235

Sample answer:

April could add $139 + 1$ to make 140, then add 27 for a sum of 167.

Warm-Up 236

Sample answer:

Brent could add $123 + 7$ to make 130, then add 40 for a sum of 170.

Warm-Up 237

Sample answers:

$20 + (6 + 4) = 30$
$(20 + 4) + 6 = 30$

Warm-Up 238

Sample answers:

$(71 + 4) + 10 = 85$
$(71 + 10) + 4 = 85$

Warm-Up 239

$12 + x = 26$ or $26 - 12 = x$

Warm-Up 240

$25 - x = 11$ or $11 + x = 25$

Warm-Up 241

10 cents

Warm-Up 242

Three packs of gum for 45 cents is a better bargain. Each pack of gum would cost 15 cents.

Warm-Up 243

$a = 4$ and $b = 4$

Warm-Up 244

$a = 4$ and $b = 3$

Warm-Up 245

1. 4 2. 5 3. 6 4. 11

Warm-Up 246

1. 6 2. 13 3. 6 4. 9

Warm-Up 247

$12 - x + 3 = 9$; $x = 6$

Warm-Up 248

$25 - 10 + x = 18$; $x = 3$

Warm-Up 249

$13 + 7 - 5 = 15$

Warm-Up 250

$9 + 9 + 9 = 27$